RELIGION AND THEATRE

RELIGION AND THEATRE

M L VARADPANDE

HUMANITIES PRESS INC.

First published 1983 in the
United States of America by
Humanities Press Inc.
Atlantic Highlands
NJ 07716

ISBN 0-391-02794-8

© M L Varadpande 1983

Cover & inside layout: Yashodamohan

All rights reserved. No part of this book may be reproduced or transmitted in any form or by any means, electronic or mechanical, including photocopying, recording or by any information storage and retrieval system, without permission in writing from the publishers.

Printed in India

To
Babasaheb and Nalini Vahini
with gratitude and affection

CONTENTS

Dedication	v
List of Illustrations	ix
Introduction	1
Religion and Theatre	5
Devadasi	45
Theatre of Bhagavatas	77
Dashavatar	90
Dance-Worship of Stupas	103
Appendix A References to Temple Theatre in Inscriptions	113
Appendix B Vanajatra: Religious Processional Theatre	120
Appendix C Children's Mystery Opera: Ras	127
Appendix D Natyacharya	133
Appendix E Shakuntala Sculptures	139
Index	145

LIST OF ILLUSTRATIONS

1. Protima Bedi on the background of wheel of Sun Temple, Konarak.
2. Ritual Dance, Bhimbetka Cave, Madhya Pradesh.
3. Worship of Bodhi Tree with song, dance and music, Sanchi.
4. Musician at Buddhist Temple, Airtam, Uzbekistan.
5. Buddhist Lama Dances, Bhutan.
6. Bhuta (Ghost) Dance, Karnataka.
7. Theyyam, Kerala.
8. Devadasi, wood sculpture from Orissa, Ashutosh Museum.
9. Stone Disk showing Devadasi, priest, temple and goddess, Rupar.
10. Devadasi and priest, steatite plaque, Rajgir.
11. Ritual copulation in yogic posture, Khajuraho.
12. Prakriti and Purush, Konarak.
13. Brihadeshvar Temple, Tanjor.
14. Mahari—temple dancer, Jagannatha Temple, Puri.
15. Devadasi dance, Hajo Temple, Assam (Reproduced from R. Nath's *The Art of Khajuraho*).
16. Swapna Sundari, Dance Festival, Khajuraho.

Courtesy: No. 2—Dr. Wakankar; Nos. 3, 8, 9, 10, 12, 13—Archaeological Survey of India; Nos. 5, 6, 7, 14—Sangeet Natak Akademi; No. 4—Times of India, Delhi; No. 1—Smt. Protima Bedi; No. 16—Smt. Swapna Sundari.

RELIGION AND THEATRE

RELIGION AND THEATRE

INTRODUCTION

A multi-dimensional relationship exists between religion and theatre.

Primitive religion is ritual oriented. A ritual is defined as a system of esoteric and sacrosanct rites with prescribed procedures. It was, and still is, performed to appease the spirits, avert calamity and set benevolent forces into action. A pronounced element of theatricality is present in rituals. Many a time a ritual takes a form of rudimentary drama. Anthropologists know that the whole hunting scene is enacted as a magico-religious ritual by the primitive community to ensure favourable results in future expeditions.

Rituals helped the inherent element of theatricality to grow and evolve itself into an independent activity.

A ritual is performed on two levels. Sometimes the whole community participates in it, and sometimes the task of performing the ritual is entrusted to persons specially chosen for the purpose. Their leader came to be known as the priest. These persons assumed different roles to act out rituals. In the priest in trance we see the early glimpse of an actor.

When, in a community, a group of persons or an individual is separated and the task of performing the ritual is entrusted to this separate group or person, there comes into existence the audience-performer division. To the arena marked out for performing a ritual the origin of the *Ranga Bhumi* (stage) can be traced. The explanatory myths generated by the rituals provided the theme for stage enactment. In the frenzied movement of the ritual performer the art of dancing originated. The gesture language adopted by the priests helped the formulation of a code of acting for the stage. The priest who acted as a medium of communication with the spirit probably created the form of verbal exchange called dialogue.

Other accessories like masks, make-up and singing are common to rituals and the theatre. Primitive religion and its system of rituals gave the dramatic art many necessary ingredients to evolve itself into a separate entity.

Even after theatre grew into an independent form, its unique relationship with religion continued taking different hues from time to time. In India this relationship is still a living reality and the mutual influences can very well be traced and discerned.

Though the history of the religion-theatre relationship goes beyond the Vedic period, we find it reflected quite clearly in the ritual of fire sacrifice of the Vedic Aryans. Vedic rituals are highly theatrical, in fact we may even call them rudimentary playlets. They incorporate in their execution song, music, dialogue, symbolic gesture language, dance, myth. All the ingredients of theatre are present in the rituals of the Vedic Aryans as they were present in the rituals of their predecessors who have left some significant evidence in the form of cave paintings.

Like the rituals, well ordained religio-philosophical

Introduction

systems and concepts have also influenced the thinking of Indian dramatists. When in his play *Mālavikāgnimitram* Kalidasa says that the drama depicts the human nature based on three fundamental qualities (*traiguṇyōdbhava lōkacharitam*), he is clearly referring to the principles of *raja*, *tama* and *satva* of Sānkhya philosophy. Likewise the categorization of men and women into three types, *uttam* (superior), *madhyam* (middling) and *adham* (inferior), made by Bharata, seems to have been based on the same fundamental qualities propounded by the Sānkhya philosophy.

The law of *Karma—Karma Siddhānta*—has deeply influenced Indian playwrights. On more than one occasion Bharata clearly states that the *karma* of people is the basic theme of the drama. It narrates actions of men (*narāṇam karmasanshrayam*), it depicts his various acts (*karmāṇi vividhāni cha*). 'I have created this science of dramaturgy taking into consideration the Karma of the people, their deeds and their emotions,' says Bharata. It is no wonder that the entire course of Indian drama was governed by the law of *Karma*. The plots of the classical Indian plays are governed by the tenets of this all-pervading religio-philosophical theory. The aim of human actions (*karma*) is to achieve four supreme goals of human existence, namely *dharma*, *artha*, *kāma* and *mōksha*. Persons who witness the dramatic performances achieve the same goals, say the dramatists.

Rasa is the aesthetic experience culminating into bliss. Drama gives this aesthetic experience to the audiences. When Vishvanatha in his work *Sāhitya*

Darpaṇa says that this blissful aesthetic experience compares with the blissful divine experience of *brahman* he is referring to the Upanishadas. The Taittirīya Upanishad says that *brahman* is *rasa* (*rasō vai sah*) and is nothing but bliss (*anandō brahmeti vyajānāt*). Achārya Nandikeshvara in his famous work *Abhinaya Darpaṇa* says that according to some scholars the blissful aesthetic experience one gets from witnessing dance or drama is superior to the blissful experience of *brahman*.

This is enough to underline the religion-theatre relationship for the present. With this in mind let us now attempt an in-depth study of this unique relationship.

RELIGION AND THEATRE

The attitude towards theatre differed from religion to religion and never remained the same even within one religion.

We know of religions which detested the theatre, negated it, but later yielded to its charm. Examples of the reverse are not also wanting. Religious teachers were afraid of the theatre. They called it a sensuous art and cautioned against its corrupting influence. However some lovingly adopted it as a medium through which the realisation of god and propagation of their faith could take place. A kind of love-hate relationship existed between these two powerful institutions. It will, therefore, be interesting to attempt a historical survey of their relationship.

The earliest extant record of dance-ritual relationship is found on the walls of the Bhimbetka cave shelters in the form of paintings belonging to the mesolithic period. In one composition three out of four dancers are seen wearing respectively a bison-horn mask, a feathered head-dress, and a wolf's head-mask. The fourth is shown taking a leap in the air. Dr Wakankar who discovered the paintings calls it a 'Wizard's Dance'. In yet another painting two figures are seen moving in a kind of trance suggestive of the ritual nature of their movements. A bison-horn mask and a feathered head-dress can be seen adorning the heads of these figures. Musical instruments like drums, cymbals, and lyres are also seen painted on the walls of Bhimbetka and other prehistoric cave shelters in the country.

These magico-religious ritualistic dances were of course performed by primitive people to appease the spirits, to cast a sympathetic magic on forthcoming events so that they could be favourable, to ensure success in hunting or war, or to ward off evil. Religion and theatre are mutually inclusive in primitive ritualistic activity motivated by community welfare. The tradition still continues in tribal societies in different regions of the country. The bison-horn head-dress on the head of the dancing figure in cave paintings, Pashupati of the Indus seal, is even today seen decorating the head of tribal dancers, and dance continues to be their ritual.

Many evidences indicate the existence of both theatrical activity and religious cults in the ancient Indus civilization that flourished from c. 2500 B.C. to 1500 B.C. A variety of masks, musical instruments, figurines of dancing men and women, and string-manipulated puppets were excavated at different sites. A seal depicting dancing to the beat of musical instruments, probably ritualistic in nature, was also found. Mackay tells that as in ancient Egypt, here too, dwarfs were kept to provide amusement and were taught to dance, in the royal and other affluent households. Mother goddesses and animal deities were worshipped. However we do not possess any conclusive evidence of the inclusion of theatrical arts in the cultic activities associated with Indus deities, though we can infer that they were part of the rituals.

The rituals of the Vedic Aryans, performed on the occasion of the fire sacrifice, were highly dramatized. The priests and performers of the fire sacrifice assumed different roles during the course of ritual, delivered dialogues with meaningful and symbolic gesticulations, sang hymns and played on musical instruments. Their books, the religious scriptures, contained myths for enactment; their hymns used for recitation at rituals were in dialogue form, and, most interesting, they had dancing gods.

The clear demarcation between dramatic ritual and dramatic entertainment is seen during the period though it must have come into existence much earlier. For instance, a regular jester-entertainer *Kari*, according to the *Vājasaneyi Samhitā* (30.6 and 20) and the *Taittirīya Brāhmana* (iii.3.10), is to be sacrificed to the deity of laughter—*Hāsa*. Probably the intention was to despatch an entertainer to heaven through the fire sacrifice, to serve the gods. Theatre operated at *yajna* ceremonies on two levels. Firstly its existence was felt through highly dramatized rituals and secondly it was fulfilling its primary obligation of entertaining people.

At the *Yajna* ceremony story-telling sessions were held, songs were sung and enacted, dances and dramas were performed. The epic Ramayana was sung at the *Yajna* of Rāma by his sons Kusha and Lava. It is significant to note that the word *Kushīlava* means actor-dancer. The Mahabharata tells us about a number of story-telling sessions and theatrical performances by actors and dancers at the *Rājasuya Yajna* performed by the Pandavas.

*Teshu te nyavasan rājan brāhmanānrupasatkrutāh
Kathayantah kathām bahvıh pashyanto naṭa
nartakān*
— MB, Sabhā, Rājasuya Parva, 33.49

The *Harivansha Purāna* records the story of an actor named Bhadra who entertained seers at the fire sacrifice conducted by Krishna's father Vasudeva.

*Tatra yajne vartamāne sunātyena naṭastada
Maharshınstoshayāmāsa Bhadranāmēti nāmatah*
— HP, Vishnu Parva, 91.26

Many scholars believe that classical Indian theatre originated in the recitation of epics like the Rāmāyana and the Mahābhārata on religious occasions. It is significant to note that Bharata says in the *Nātya Shāstra* that a story taken from the Vedic lore for enactment is called drama.

An interesting stone panel ascribed to A.D. 500, housed in Gwalior Museum, depicts the various facets of Bali's *Yajna*. Explaining it C. Shivaramamurthi in his book *Natarāja* says:

> Dance is not only a pleasurable ocular sacrifice but also a popular happy adjunct to the regular sacrifice itself. Dance and music, particularly the chant of *Sōma* hymns to the tune of *Vīna*, was an essential factor of *Yāgas*.
> One of the most graphic representations of Trivikrama's triumph over Bali on a Gupta architrave from Pavaya, now in the Gwalior Museum, illustrates this very clearly in an elaborate series of panels depicting various facets of Bali's *Yāga* with horse stationed at *Yūpa* post, the

princes watching from near the *Yajna Vāṭa*, the *Ritwik* priests assembled, the musical orchestra as an accompaniment to dance.

The variation of the shape of *Vīna* is also shown there, the guitar like *Kacchapi* and the bow shaped *Saptatantri*. The threefold drum is also there, *Tripuskara* as it is called, and the dancer's movement is a delicate stance of *Angahāra*.

The famous dance scene itself is a part of the celebration of Bali's *Yāga*.

The evolution of theatrical arts as an integral part of the ritual and as an independent form of entertainment is discernible from the evidence recorded till now. One must be very clear that we are not discussing here the issue of secular *vs* religious origin of theatre. Origin of theatrical arts cannot be attributed to a single source and same is the case of religion. We are merely exploring their mutual relationship and influences, and find that both enriched each other substantially, significantly. But it is not that religion always supported theatre; there are instances, in fact, when theatre ridiculed religion.

It was the early ascetic Buddhism which came out strongly against the theatrical arts and strictly prohibited the celibate monks from witnessing dance, drama, and even music performances. According to the *Lalit Vistara*, Buddha himself was adept in 'the art of Vīna, all manner of instrumental music, dance, song, recitation, *lāsya*, comic and dramatic action'. He appeared to witness, according to *Lalit Vistara*, the 'drama of Great Law'. He did not much approve of the stage-shows. In the *Dīggha Nikaya*, Bhagawān

Buddha specifically states that Gotama the recluse refrains from being a spectator at shows, at fairs with *Nauch* dances, singing and music. In the *Magghima Sila* of the same book he regretfully says: 'Whereas some recluses and Brahmans, while living on the food provided by the faithful, continue addicted to visiting shows; that is to say dances (*nākkam*), singing of songs (*gītam*), instrumental music (*vāditam*), ballad recitation or story telling (*ākhyānam*), hand music (*pāṇissaram*), scenery used for ballet-dance (*sōbhanāgarakam*), dramatic shows (*pēkkham*), chanting of bards (*vētālam*) . . .'

Not only did he talk against the monks attending dramatic shows and theatrical performances but he acted sternly when it became necessary. The *Avadānshataka* tells us the story of Kuvalaya, the proud and beautiful daughter of the Dance Teacher of Dakshinapatha, who tried to entice monks by a frank exhibition of her lovely body while dancing. Angry, Buddha punished her by turning her into a hideous creature.

Vinaya Texts tell us about two monks Assangi and Punabbasu and their over-indulgence in theatrical entertainments. They were termed as wicked and shameless as they used to dance, and sing and play music. Once these monks from Kita hills visited a theatre. Spreading their robes they invited the dancer to dance on it. They were unceremoniously expelled from the order for their unruly behaviour.

The people also reacted sharply when they found some monks enjoying themselves at theatrical performances. The *Chullavagga* says that once monks went to see dramatic performances which were held on a mountain (*Giragga Samagga*) near Rajagaha. Says the book:

> The people murmured, were annoyed and became indignant saying, 'How can the Sākhyaputtiya Samanas go to see dancing and singing and music like those who are still enjoying the pleasures of the world?' When this matter was reported to the Blessed One he admonished them by saying: 'You are not, O Bhikkus, to go to see dancing or singing or music. Whosoever does so shall be guilty of a *dukkhata*.'

It was natural for the Buddha to restrain the monks from participation in sensuous arts but Emperor Ashoka who came under the influence of Buddhism even tried to ban theatrical arts. In his rock edict he says:

> Here not a single living creature should be slaughtered and sacrificed. Nor should any Samaja be held. For His Sacred and Gracious Majesty sees much objection in such Samaja. But there are certain varieties of the same which are considered commendable by His Sacred and Gracious Majesty . . .

Commenting upon the edict Dr Radhakumud Mookerji in his book *Ashoka* says:

> The objectionable kind of Samaja is described in the *Dīgha Nikaya* (Vol. iii, p. 183, P.T.S.) as comprising six features of 'dancing, singing, music, story telling, cymbals and tam-tams'. Again the *Brahmajala Sutta* (Digha, i, p. 6) mentions several objectionable shows (*visuka-dassanam*) marked by some of the above features. One of these is called *pekkham* which Buddhaghosha has explained as *nata-samajja*.

Dr D.R. Bhandarkar opines that objectionable kind of Samāja includes one in which animal slaughter used to take place in addition to theatrical entertainments. Considering Buddha's stern opposition to theatrical arts one can safely conclude that Ashoka wanted to ban theatre in his domain.

How much and why Buddha was against the theatrical arts can best be judged from the story of Talaputa which comes in the 19th canto of *Theragatha*. Talaputa was the leader of a troupe of actors. There were five hundred actresses in his company. Once he requested the Master to comment upon the belief that the actor who amuses his audiences is reborn after death among the gods of laughter. The Master caustically said: 'Director, those persons who induce sensual, misanthropic or mentally confused states in others and cause them to lose earnestness will, after death, be reborn in purgatory.' It was natural for Ashoka to see many objectionable things in Samaja—theatrical festivity.

However, the question remains as to which varieties of Samaja His Gracious Majesty considered as commendable? In his rock edict No. IV he advocates the organisation of 'shows and processions exhibiting images of gods in their celestial cars which were accompanied by elephants, fireworks and heavenly scenes.' These types of religious Samajas might have been favoured by the Emperor.

However it is significant to note that well before Ashoka's time the tradition of staging plays based on the life of Buddha had come into vogue. Though Buddha negated theatre, the theatre adopted him.

The *Avadānshataka* records that a certain Natacharya from Dakshinapatha staged before the king of Shobhāvati a *'Buddha Nātaka'* in which he himself acted as Buddha. The king was so pleased with the performance that he rewarded the Natacharya and his troupe with a lot of money.

One of the early Sanskrit dramatists wrote a play *Sariputraprakarana* on the Buddhist theme. There are evidences to show that this play used to be performed in the Buddhist monasteries of Mathura. Fa-hsien says:

> Actors were hired to perform a play in which Sariputra who was originally Brahmin goes to Buddha to ask for ordination. The lives of Maudgalyaputra and Kasyapa are also performed in this way (in Mathura) (Quoted by Kunjunni Raja in his book *Kūṭiyāttam*, Chinese Literature, part 3, p. 149).

Another Chinese pilgrim I-tsing (671-695 A.D.) says:

> King Siladitya versified the story of the Bōdhisattava Jīmūtavāhana (Chinese: 'Cloud-Borne') who surrendered himself in the palace of a Naga. This version was set to music (Lit : string and pipe). He had it performed by a band accompanied by dancing and acting, thus popularising it (A Record of Buddhist Religion as Practised in India, p. 163-4).

Obviously he is referring to the play *Nāgānanda* written by King Harsha.

Commenting upon the Ratnagiri copper-plate inscription of Somavanshi King Karna who flourished in Orissa about the beginning of the 12th century A.D., D.C. Sircar writes:

> We have found some proof to show that Devadasis were maintained in the early medieval period not only in Brahmanical temples but also in Buddhist shrines at least in Eastern India ... Karpurashri had really been a Devadasi attached to the Buddhist temple in Mahāvihāra at Salonpura (Ep. Ind., Vol. 35, p. 97-98).

An inscription at the Sun Temple near Visnupāda at Gaya speaks of a Buddhist temple where beautiful Bhāvinis and Chētis used to dance accompanied by instrumental music (Indian Antiquary, December 1881, Vol. X, p. 341-347).

Explaining the Buddhist inscription, dated in the year 1813 of Buddha Nirvana, Pandit Bhagvanlal Indraji opines that the temple may have originally been a Buddhist one, but having been deserted under the Mohammadans, the Brahmans may have imported into it an image of Surya. The inscription opens with the words *Om namo Buddhāya shuddhāya namo dharmāya*. Its 12th line clearly says:

> Since in the religion of Bhagavat, worship is here (offered) to the most worshipful one, always three times a day, by means of instrumental music in the highest key, together with Bhāvinis and Chētis dancing around wonderfully.

Temple girls, beautiful like nymph Rambha (*Rambhāsannibha*), used to perform captivating dances (*Tyatbhutam nrityāni*) with songs in honour of the Bhagavat.

Religion and Theatre

In his work *Chu-fan-chi* the Chinese traveller Chau Ju-Kwa who visited India in the 12th century mentions songs sung in honour of Buddha at a Buddhist establishment in Gujarat. He says:

> Four thousand Buddhist temple buildings in which live over twenty thousand who sing twice daily while offering food to Buddha (i.e. the idols) and while offering flowers (Ocean of Stories, p. 241).

It seems that the tradition of staging plays on the Buddhist theme was prevalent in eastern India also. The *Charja-Pada*, a collection of Buddhist verses dated 10th-12th century of Christian era, allegorically speaks of Buddha Nātaka. It says:

> *Nāchanti bājila gānti devi*
> *Buddha nātaka bisama hoi*

Describing the grandeur of the divine play a *Pada* states:

> Sun is the tumba of Vina, moon is the string, rod is shūnyata (nothingness). This divine anāhat Vīna (lyre) is being played and the sound of nothingness emitted from the strings is pervading the Universe. Ali and Kali are two tunes and mind is the joint. When pressed with the palm of the hand and the strings are struck, music starts flowing. Everything is filled with the majestic sound of thirty-two strings. Bajradhar dances, Dēvi sings and this way Buddha Nātaka is being enacted.

It would be quite interesting to mention in this context a Buddhist work *Saddharma Pundarīka* written a few centuries before the birth of Christ. Its semi-dramatic format made scholars think that it was probably written for stage presentation. H. Kern while writing an introduction to its English translation observes:

> The *Lalita Vistāra* has the movement of real epic, the *Saddharma Pundarīka* has not. The latter bears the character of a dramatic performance, an undeveloped mystery play, in which the chief interlocutor is Sākyamuni, the Lord. It consists of a series of dialogues, brightened by the magic effects of a would-be supernatural scenery. The phantasmagorical parts of the whole are as clearly intended to impress us with the idea of the might and glory of the Buddha, as his speeches are to set forth his all-surpassing wisdom. Some affinity of its technical arrangement with that of the regular Indian drama is visible in the prologue or Nidāna, where Manjushri at the end prepares the spectators and auditors—both are the same—for the beginning of the grand drama, by telling them that the Lord is awake from his mystic slumber, to display his infinite wisdom and power (The Sacred Books of the East, Vol. XXI).

This is indeed a very interesting observation. However we do not have any positive proof, except for its format, which indicates that the work was put on the stage by actors. However the *Saddharma Pundarīka* gives us very significant information about the mode of Stupa worship. Stupa is a dome-shaped monument containing relics of the Buddha or other similar dignitaries. The book says:

> They are always decorated with flags, a multitude of bells is constantly heard sounding; men, gods, goblins and

Religion and Theatre

titans offer worship with flowers, perfume and music.

If the scenes sculpted on the stone railings, gateways of stupas at Bharhut, Sanchi or Amaravati are indicative of religious practices of contemporary Buddhism, we may safely conclude that the religion was not averse to theatrical arts. We have already learnt from *Saddharma Pundarīka* that music formed a part of stupa worship. These sculptures tell us that in addition to music other theatrical arts like dancing, singing, play-acting were also included in the ritual of worshipping the stupa. A fine Sanchi panel shows a Naga king worshipping Buddha in his symbolic Bodhi tree form with a band of dancers, singers and musicians. At Bharhut a dance party is shown performing in veneration to Buddha's head-dress—Chūdamaha. On the Prasēnjit pillar of the same stupa enactment of an opera before a Bodhi tree is shown. Names of the dancers are also inscribed. In one of the Amaravati sculptures we find a person carrying Buddha's relics on his head followed by a procession of dancers, singers and musicians.

There are several such sculptures adorning Buddhist monuments all over the country. The picture galleries of Ajanta depict dance scenes in abundance. This clearly shows that people used to offer dance, drama, music and songs to Buddha during the festive worship of stupa which contained his relics. It is significant to note that at Airtam in the southern Uzbekistan a relief showing busts of three musicians against the background of *scanthus* leaves was found. This relic of the Kushan era once

adorned the entrance to a Buddhist temple.
In the Buddhist Vihara complex excavated at
Nagarjunakonda in Andhra Pradesh a unique amphi-
theatre was found, connected by a flight of steps to
the temple of a Buddhist deity, Hariti, with the
Triratna mark. The possibility of Buddhist plays
being performed in this amphi-theatre belonging to
the 3rd century A.D. cannot be ruled out. A detailed
information about this structure is given in the book
Traditions of Indian Theatre.

As the influence of Buddhism started waning the
Buddhist theatre suffered a setback. However the
tradition survived in the Himalayan regions where
the religion retained its hold. Even today the Lama
Buddhist monasteries stage plays on Buddhist themes
during festivities. In Tibet Jataka stories were also
enacted. Various ritualistic mask dances were performed signifying the victory of good over evil.
These mystery plays have still retained their ritualistic
significance. Sylvain Levi in his book on Indian
theatre has given some information about the performance of Buddhist plays in Tibet.
He says:

> The Buddhist monasteries in Tibet have preserved the
> custom of staging miracle-plays twice a year, once during
> the spring festival and once during the autumn festival. In
> those plays the roles of the good spirits are taken by the
> monks and those of the evil spirits by lay people. All the
> actors wear strange and richly decorated costumes and
> masks. The plays open with the benediction sung by the
> whole cast. Then one evil spirit enters and tries to entice
> by discourses and jokes a poor mortal who finds it

difficult to resist the temptation. At that moment friends come to the rescue of the tempted man. The evil spirit summons his companions and a violent struggle ensues. The mortals desperately invoke the help of the good spirits who come down and put the evil spirits to flight. The evil spirits are pushed and pitilessly beaten. This kind of spectacle is a strange blending of theological controversies and vulgar farce, bringing together characters of both popular and religious drama. The monks do not know the origin of those plays. They stage them to be faithful to an ancient tradition. The conservatism of religious institutions allow us to see in these modern miracle-plays a faithful picture of the pious spectacles performed in the ancient monasteries of India.

Levi also refers to Buddhist theatre tradition in Burma, China and Ceylon. We find this tradition still alive in the monasteries of Bhutan, Ladakh and other Himalayan regions. During its long existence Buddhism came down from complete negation to total acceptance of theatre. This probably was effected under the influence of folk religious cults whose mode of worship included offerings of music, dance, drama to appease their deities. With the passage of time the strict asceticism of early Buddhism started relaxing in many respects. For instance in early Buddhist art the Master was represented symbolically. A pair of feet, the wheel of law or the Bodhi tree indicated his presence. Slowly this symbolism was replaced by beautiful anthropomorphic representations of Buddha in sitting or standing postures, probably under the Greek influence, or as a result of art activity of the Mathura school of Indian art. This process of visualisation naturally took Buddhism to a still more visual or audio-visual art form viz., theatre.

Another Indian religious sect which is not much enthusiastic about theatre is of course Jainism. However it did not neglect it with the same vehemence as Buddhism did. Many Jain literary works speak of play enactment, theatre halls, dance and music. Ancient temples of Jinas used to vibrate with the dancing feet of beautiful girls. A very enchanting sculpture of a danseuse in the act of putting on an anklet adorns a Jain temple at Khajuraho. It can be counted among the masterpieces of Indian art. Let us now turn to Jain theatre tradition.

We find an elaborate description of thirty-two types of dramatic representations in the Jain work *Rajaprashniya Sutra*. Many terms that occur in this context are similar to those of *Natyashastra* of Bharata. The classification includes imitation of gaits of different animals, movements of sun and moon, various types of dance formations, and acrobatic movements of various types. It also includes an enactment of Bhagavan Mahavira's life from birth to death. We may infer on the basis of the evidence provided by the work that the tradition of presenting plays depicting the lives of the Jain Tirthankaras was in vogue in ancient India.

A Jain monk named Asādhabhuti wrote a play on the life of the monarch Bharata. It was staged at Pataliputra, says the *Pinda Niryukti*. The play so powerfully projected the philosophy of asceticism that many kings abandoned their kingdoms after witnessing it. Fearing that no Kshatriya will remain to rule the earth if this continued to happen, the play was destroyed. This is a good example of how theatre can be a medium of propagation of religious philosophy. And precisely for the same reason theatre was adopted by religious sects.

Epigraphical and literary references indicate that courtesans and dancers who were custodians of theatrical arts in ancient India were devoted to Jain religion. They paid their homage to *Jinas*, constructed shrines in their honour, and invoked them during difficult times. Thus reads a 1st century B.C. inscription in the Mathura Museum:

> Adoration to the *Arhat Vardhamana*. The daughter of the matron (?) courtesan Lonasobhika, the disciple of the ascetics, the junior (?) courtesan Vasu has erected a shrine to the Arhat, a hall of homage (*ayagasabha*), a cistern (and) a stone slab at the sanctuary of the *Nirgrantha Arhata*, together with her mother, (her sister), her daughter, her son and her whole household, in honour of the Arhata.

The word *shobhika* occurs in the *Mahābhāshya* of Patanjali in the sense of an actor. Kaiyyata says it denotes a dance-master. The same term occurs in the above mentioned inscription. Were these actresses enacting Jain lore at Mathura?

A very interesting fragment of a running frieze containing a dancing scene was recovered from the Kankali tila of Mathura. Now housed in the Lucknow Museum, it dates back to 2nd century B.C. Here the Apsara Nīlanjana is shown dancing before the first Jain Tirthankara, Rishabhadeva. This supports our conclusion that Mathura actresses used to enact Jain lore.

In a Jain work *Vasudeva Hindi* it is narrated how a danseuse invoked Jinas to save her from poisoned needles while dancing. It says:

> Once the hermits Vadava, Sandiki, Udayabindu and others approached the king with flowers and fruits. They said to him, 'There is going to be a sacrifice-ceremony in the hermitage and you are able to give protection.'
> King asked the prince to protect them and the prince went to the hermitage with army.
> While ceremony was going on, the prostitutes Cittasena, Kalingasena, Angasena and Kamapadaga were giving their performance in the spirit of competition (*sanghansaena*).
> Dumuha waited for Kamapadaga's turn and then he ordered her to show needle-dance (*suinatta*). He applied poison to the needles and put them under her dancing feet.
> When Kamapadaga became aware of this, she propitiated the deity by declaring, 'If I overcome this difficult situation, I shall celebrate the eight-day festival (*atthahiya*) in honour of the Jinas. She succeeded in her performance and the poisoned needles had been removed by the deity (WH 281, 23-283, 25 Tr. J.C. Jain).

The Jain monarch of Orissa, Kharavela, in his Hathigumpha cave inscription records the celebration of a dramatic festival (*Samaja*) full of singing, dancing and music. Hathigumpha is one of the ancient Jain caves excavated on the twin hills of Udayagiri and Khandagiri. In the same cave complex is located the Jain Rani Gumpha cave which was the venue of the *Samaja* conducted by Kharavela. The inscription tells us that the monarch himself was adept in theatrical arts. He must have encouraged the enactment of Jain lore at *Samaja* festivals organised by him.

We have evidences to indicate that dances were performed, and plays were enacted before the idols of the Tirthankaras in the Jain temples. The Jain temples at Halebid in Karnataka have been provided with beautiful Navaranga halls with circular dancing floors and exquisitely carved and polished pillars. Queen Shantala, adept in Bharatnatyam, used to perform before the magnificent images of Tirthankaras in these 12th century temples. It is said that she remained a devout Jain, though her husband Vishnuvardhana adopted the Bhagavata cult.

Jalore (Rajasthan) stone inscription of Samarasimha Deva tells us about the construction of Shri Kuvaravihara by Chalukya Kumarapala in Vikram Samvat 1221. It was renovated by Chahamana Samarasimha in v.s. 1242. To honour Lord Mahavira a *torana* was constructed and a golden staff for hoisting flags was offered by the royal family in v.s. 1256. The most important reference is to the setting up of the golden cupola in the newly built central hall for dramatic performances on the occasion of *Diptosava Dana* in v.s. 1268. The inscription written in Sanskrit clearly points out a tradition, in the Jain Viharas, of performing plays on festive occasions before the idol of Mahavira (*Ep. Ind.*, Vol. XI, p. 54-55).

There is a beautiful music hall attached to Vardhamana or Trailokyanath temple at Tiruparuttikunram (Jain Kanchi). A temple inscription says that the Maha Mandapa for musical concerts (*Mahamandapam Samgıtārtham*) was built at the instance of Pushpasena in the year 1387-88 by General Irugappa, son of General Vaichaya (*Bulletin of Madras Govt. Museum*, Vol. I, Part III, 1934, p. 57). It may be mentioned here that the word '*Sangita*' had a wider connotation and it included dance, music, singing and even theatrical enactment.

In Jain literature we find elaborate description of a theatre hall. Writing about it Shri Jain says:

> We learn about the theatre hall (*picchagharamandava*) which was supported by many columns (*anegakhambhasayasannivittha*), and was furnished with huge altars (*vedika*), arches (*torana*) and *shalabhanjika* figures; it was decorated with *Ihamriga* etc., was fitted with a mechanism to show the moving figures of the pair of *Vidyadharas* had hundreds of figures decorating it, had many domes (*thubhiya*), was decorated with flags and bells, was well plastered and bore the palm impression inside and outside; its gates had sandal pitchers and arches; there were flowers, garlands, perfumes and incense, and the ceiling was decorated with lotus creepers. In the centre of the theatre hall there was a stage (*akkhadaga*) which had a jewelled seat (*manipedhiya*) in the centre. On that there was a throne having discs (*cakkala*), lions, feet (*paya*), tops and body and joint (Rayapaseniya, 41f).

In the ancient Jain text in Prakrit, *Tiloyapannatti*, we find a description of a *Nattyasala* – a theatre hall with thirty-two platforms with thirty-two dancers dancing on them and singing songs in honour of Tirthankaras. In the *Adipurana* of Bhagavat Jinasenacharya there is a mention of two theatre halls

Religion and Theatre

which looked as if the earth was holding them with great devotion for worshipping Jinendra Bhagavan (with theatricals).

In the Jain works we find the mention of *Raspekkhana*—the *Ras* plays. Some scholars think that Vaishnava *Ras* tradition was inspired by the *Ras* performances of the Jain Sravakas and women devotees, in the Jain temples around 14th century. However Vaishnava *Ras* tradition is much older. Jain Acharyas of Rajasthan composed several operatic *Ras* plays for enactment in temples before the congregation of devotees. Full of dancing, singing and music these Jain *Ras* plays were performed by professional actors also. These plays were mainly based upon the lives of their religious leaders (Tirthankaras), Jain saints, and ideal devotees. Many Jain Munis opposed the enactment of these plays in the temples and ultimately Jain temple theatre tradition practically came to an end.

However it is interesting to note that these *Ras* plays were performed as an offering to the deities and were considered sacred. It is written in the *Ravantgiri Ras* that 'whosoever will enthusiastically enact this *Ras* play will be blessed by Jina Neminatha and goddess Ambika will fulfil all his desires' (*Vraj Ka Sanskritik Itihas*: Prabhudayal Mittal). This attitude of looking at dramatic arts is in conformity with Indian theatre tradition. Bharata states in his *Natyashastra*:

> The gods are never so pleased on being worshipped with scents and garlands, as they are delighted with the performance of dramas. The man who properly attends the

performance of music or dramas, will (after his death) attain the happy and meritorious path in the company of Brahmanic sages (XXXVI.81-82).

The Jain writers wrote some interesting plays, two of which have been mentioned by A. Berriedale Keith in his work *The Sanskrit Drama*. *Kaumudimitrananda* is a romantic comedy with a complicated plot by 12th century Jain writer Ramachandra. Another play of the same period is *Prabhuddharawhaneya* written by Ramabhadra Muni. It is significant to note that this play with six acts was specially written by the Jain monk for performing in the temple of Yugadideva or Tirthankar Rishabha on the occasion of *Jatra* festival. This reminds us of the Hindu tradition of presenting plays at the time of temple festivals: *Jatras*. It is a well known fact that Bhavabhuti wrote his plays *Mahaviracharitam*, *Uttarramcharitam* and *Malatimadhavam* for performance at the *Jatra* of Kalapriyanath. Bhana Ubayabhisarika mentions the enactment of an opera *Sangitak* named *Madanārādhan* in the temple of Bhagawan Vishnu. Presenting plays on the occasion of temple festivals was, and still is, a common practice.

Not only did Jain writers write plays, but they also wrote treatises on dramaturgy. In the 11th century, Anhilpattan in Gujarat was a great centre of Jain culture. Hemachandra was a famous Jain Acharya of the time. His disciple Ramachandra in collaboration with another scholar, Gunachandra, wrote a book *Nātyadarpan* which is considered one of the major works on Indian dramaturgy. In the benedictory verse of the treatise the authors have expressed their reverence to Jina Vani—teachings of Jain Acharyas—which helps people to attain the four goals of human life that is *dharma, artha, kāma* and *mōksha*:

> *Chaturvarga phala nityam*
> *Jaini vāchamupāsmahe*
> *Rūpairdwādashabhir-vishvam*
> *Yayā nyāyyē ghrutam pathi*

The authors say that Jina Vani assumes twelve forms. Likewise there are twelve types of drama. In the opening verse of the *Dasharupaka* the author Dhananjaya has compared ten forms of drama with ten incarnations of Vishnu. This is a very interesting example of how the religious concepts of the writers of these treatises have influenced their works.

Deities of the Hindu pantheon are fond of theatrical arts. Shiva is called the supreme dancer — Nataraj. The most magnificent description of Shiva, the Nataraj occurs in the *Abhinaya Darpana* of Achārya Nandikeshvara. It says:

> *Āngikam bhuvanam yasya*
> *Vāchikam sarva vāngmayam*
> *Āhāryam chandratārādi*
> *Tam namah Sātvikam Shivam*

The entire universe is his physical entity and all its activity nothing but a manifestation of his acting, entire literature is his *Vachikabhinaya* or theatrical speech, his make-up is done with dazzling celestial bodies like moon and stars. O Satvika Shiva, I bow before thee!

The Indian works on theatre believe in the fourfold division of acting – *Āngika* (physical), *Vāchika* (verbal), *Āhārya* (make-up, stage decor etc.) and *Sātvika* (emotive content of theatrical arts). Shiva is described here as an embodiment of all these four principles.

Ritualistic worship of Shiva includes theatrical arts. Pashupata sect of Shaivism enjoins its followers to resort to *Hasit*, *Gita*, and *Nritya* as a part of worship to appease Shiva. *Hasit* is a peculiar type of laughter. According to Bharata the *pramatha ganas* — dwarfish attendants of Shiva—are the deities of the sentiment of laughter. These *ganas* in various humorous moods are sculpted on the Bhumara temple.

Then comes *Gita* which means singing songs according to musicology, narrating the stories of Shiva. These songs enacted through dancing is *Nritya*. Pāshupat Āchāryas were found in the company of courtesans and dancing girls. The *Kuttanimatam* tells us that pāshupatāchārya Bhāvashuddha built a magnificent mansion for a dancer named Anangadevi (V, 538). A customer tauntingly calls a dancing girl 'Āchāryāni' because she was found moving in the company of a Pāshupat Āchārya. Probably these Āchāryas needed dancers for the ritualistic Shiva worship.

The *Shākta* cult of Shaivism seems to believe in

appeasing the supreme actor with performance of theatrical arts. The Yogini temple at Hirapur in Orissa provides an interesting evidence. In the centre is a Shiva shrine. There is a circular enclosure in which are fitted exquisite sculptures of Yoginis in various alluring dancing postures. It is evident that this unusual circular shrine was used for esoteric *Shākta* rituals which included dancing in some form.

It is very interesting to note that ritualistic gestures are known as *Mudras* and the same term is used to indicate gestures in dancing and in acting. Many scholars feel that ritualistic *Mudras* are the source of theatrical gesture-language symbolism.

It is also significant to note that the opening benedictory verses of majority of classical Sanskrit plays are dedicated to Shiva. Plays were enacted at Shiva temples on festive occasions. It seems that the system of *devadāsis*, temple dancing girls, was greatly encouraged by the Shaiva cult. According to inscriptional evidence, a majority of the four hundred dancing girls that the Chola king Rājarāja employed to serve Lord Shiva at the Brihadeshvar temple of Tanjore were drawn from other Shiva temples in the region. The Kalajar temple inscription records the name of the chief *devadāsi* and the guard attached to the temple. It says:

Deva (?) Sri Nilakaṇṭha
ma (?) nityam pranamati
Aum! Sam 1186 Maharaja Sri
Madana Varma Deva II maha
Pratihara Sangrama Sinha II

Maha nāchani Padāmavati

It is significant to note that all the 108 dancing units known as *karanas* are depicted on the Gopuram of the Chidambaram Shiva temple according to the description given by Bharata. The cult of Shiva made significant contribution to the development of Indian theatre, and particularly dance.

In the *Sabha Parva* of the *Mahābhārata* there is a description of assembly halls of different deities. In the beautiful *Indra Sabha* we find the king of heaven being entertained with songs, dances and musical instruments, by the *apsaras* and the *gandharvas*.

*Tathaivāpsaraso rājangandharvāscha manoramah
Nrityavāditragitaischa hasyaischa vividhairapi*

Mahābhārata mentions that humorous entertainment was also arranged for Indra.

In the assembly hall of the dreadful god of the dead, Yama, theatrical performances, humorous entertainments, and charming dances (*lāsya*) went on.

*Gandharvāscha mahātmanah sanghashaschāpsaroganah
Vāditram nrityagitamcha hāsyam lāsyam cha sarvashah*

Varuna, the deity of water, is worshipped by *gandharvas* and *apsaras* by singing and dancing. The same atmosphere is there in the *Sabha* of Kubera, treasurer of gods and supreme deity of *Yakshas*,

Religion and Theatre

Gandharvas and *Apsaras*. Beautiful dancing apsaras include Mishrakēshi, Rambhā, Chitrasena, Ghritāchi and Mēnaka.

The most magnificent *Sabha* is that of Brahma, the god of creation and knowledge. According to Indian tradition it was Brahma who gave *Nātyashāstra* to Bharata. In his assembly drama, poetry, story, etc., await enactment for his recreation.

Nātakā vividhāh kāvyāh kathākyaikhārika
Tatra tishtanti tē punyā ye chānye gurupujakā

All the lines quoted above support the contention that gods are most pleased by theatrical performances like dance, drama and music. They also recognise the importance of theatrical arts in religion and religious rituals.

Indian tradition, as recorded in the *Natyashastra* of Bharata, believes in the divine origin of theatre. Brahma created the science of drama; Shiva, the Lord of Himalayas, and his charming consort Parvati embellished its performance with forceful and delicate modes of dancing; Vishnu created dramatic styles. *Apsaras*, heavenly danseuses, enacted the female roles. However, Bharata does not fail to record that it was the synthesis of divine and human efforts which finally resulted in the emergence of the theatre. God created the art, man executed it.

The first ever dramatic performance, according to Indian tradition, was on the occasion of the banner festival of Indra—*Dhwaja Maha Sriman Mahēndrasya*. Indra is a mighty god of thunder, cloud and rain. His association with theatrical arts dates back to Rig Vedic times. Rig Veda describes him as a dancer. Dramatic character of the deity is very well reflected in some of the dialogue hymns in the book, which according to many scholars were the early dramatic texts. He is seen delivering a grandiose monologue under the influence of intoxicating *Soma* juice (X.10.7) and also in conversation with his charming, vivacious wife Indrani and his pet monkey *Vrishakapi* (X.7.2). These dialogues, some scholars think, were delivered at the time of fire sacrifice by the priest, assuming different roles. In the Puranic literature he is portrayed as a deity fond of dancing and singing. It was proper to include theatrical performances at the celebrations held in his honour. We find many references in the ancient literature of how his festival used to be marked by theatrical activities.

Indra's banner festival is described in detail in the Adi parva of the *Mahabharata*. Pleased by the penance of King Uparichar Vasu, Indra gave him a bamboo pole. On New Year's day, Pratipada, the king placed it on a high pedestal, decorated it with cloth, flowers, sandal paste and jewellery, and organised a festival, *Maha*, in honour of Indra. It is considered that this festival makes the entire nation victorious and prosperous. On Bharata's testimony we can say that dramatic performances formed part of this religious festival.

The famous Tamil epic *Shilappadhikāram*, written in the second century A.D., also refers to a dramatic festival held in honour of Indra and his son Jayanta in the southern countries. In the fifth chapter of the epic it is said that the festival was full of singing, dancing and music. It hummed with the 'melodies produced by the flute, the drum, the stringed musical instrument called *Yal* and singing of songs by a class of minstrels and music masters called *pānar*.' The most interesting account of worshipping the flag staff which represented the son of Indra, and planting it ceremoniously on the stage, is given in the third canto of the epic.

> On the day (of the dramatic performance) on which this staff (representing Jayanta, son of Indra) was to be used, the dancing girl had to bathe it with holy waters brought in a golden pitcher, and afterwards garland it. Then it was handed over with blessings to the state elephant already adorned with a plate of gold and other ornaments on its forehead. To the accompaniment of the drum proclaiming victory and other musical instruments, the king and his five groups of advisers circumambulated the chariot and the elephant and gave the pole to the musician-poet on the top of the chariot. They then went round the town in a procession, and entering the theatre, placed the pole in its appropriate position.

This reminds us of the procession of Dionysius and the planting of his symbol or image in the theatre before the commencement of performances. A Greek vase painting suggests that a mask or image of Dionysius hoisted on a pole also used to be taken out in procession. This indicates the relationship of religious festivity and theatre in ancient civilizations.

A festival of Indra full of dance, drama and music is mentioned in a Jain work *Uttaradhyayana commentary*. The festival, which lasted for seven days, was celebrated by king Dummuha in Kampillapura. Writing about this Shri Jain says:

> The banner of Indra (Indakeu) was raised amidst loud and auspicious cries, which was flagged with white banners adorned with a number of little bells, covered with beautiful wreaths and garlands, decorated with a string of jewels and decked with pendant mass of various fruits. Then dancing girls performed their dance, poetic compositions were sung, people danced, wonderful feats were shown by jugglers, drums were sounded.

Ritualistic worship of popular folk and tribal deities invariably includes the elements of dance, drama and music. Bharata has clearly acknowledged this fact in his *Natyashastra*. Explaining how the various preliminaries of the play please different deities he states:

> The *pratyahara* (arranging the musical instruments) pleases the Rākshasas and the Pannagas, while the apsaras are delighted with the *avatarana* (singers taking position on the stage). The gandharvas are pleased when the *ārambha* (commencement of vocal exercise for singing) is performed and in the performance of the *āshrāvana* (adjusting the musical instruments in due manner) the Daityas take delight. The *raktrapani* (rehearsing the different styles of playing musical instruments) pleases the Dānavas and in the *parighattana* (adjusting the strings of instruments) the hosts of Rākshasas are (again) pleased. By the *samghotana* (use of different hand-poses for indicating the time beat) Guhyakas are satisfied, while the *mārgasārita* (playing together of drums and musical instruments) pleases the Yakshas. When songs (*gīta*) are sung the gods are pleased

and Rudra with his followers is pleased by the performance of the *vardhamāna* (a class of songs with dance). In the performance of walking round (by the director by praising deities) Lokapālas are delighted and the Moon-God is pleased by the benediction (*Nāndi*). During the singing of *avakrsta* (*Dhruva*) Nāgas are pleased, while Sukāvakrsta (Dhruva with meaningless sound) pleases the hosts of pitars (ancestors). In the *rangadvāra* (commencement of performance which includes words and gestures) Vishnu is pleased while *jarjara* ceremony pleases the leaders of *vighnas* (obstacles). On the *chāri* being performed (delicate movements depicting erotic sentiments) Umā takes pleasure while in the performance of *mahāchāri* (movements delineating the furious sentiments—furious dance) the Bhūtas are delighted (NS, V. 45-54).

These words of Bharata reflect the ancient ritualistic tradition of god worship with dance and music. For instance the Yaksha was worshipped with flowers, incense, wine and music. Beautiful Yakshis in alluring dancing poses decorate many ancient monuments including gates and railings of Buddhist stupas. Referring to the Tamil epic *Jīvaka Chintamani*, Dr. Anand Coomarswamy states:

> The grateful Jīvaka erected a temple for Yakkha Sutānjana, set up a statue and dedicated a town (the rent whereof would support the service of the temple). Then he prepared a drama relating to the history of the Yaksha and most likely we would understand that this drama was performed in the temple on special occasions for the pleasure of the deity. The tutelary Yaksha at Vaishali, as we have seen, was worshipped with oblations, dance and song and sound of musical instruments.

In *Aupapatika Sutra* there is an elaborate description of the shrine of Yaksha Pūrnabhadra which was always 'haunted by dancers, actors, jugglers, acrobats, jesters, jumpers, singers, story-tellers, pole-dancers, picture-showmen (*mankha*), pipers, lute players, rope-walkers, boxers, wrestlers and minstrels.' In folk-tales *yakshinis* in the guise of beautiful dancers are seen enticing traders and finally devouring them. Jatras full of theatrical entertainment were held in honour of *yakshas*. Similar festivals were held in honour of other folk deities. Thus, religious festivals were full of dramatic entertainment. The more significant fact is that dance and music found place in religious rituals themselves.

In ancient India theatrical festivities were held in honour of different deities. Some of these festivals are still in vogue. They were called *Maha, Jatra, Utsava* or *Samaja*. Like the Yaksha festival there was the *Nadi Jatra* (river-festival), *Naga Jatra, Giri Maha, Chaitya Jatra, Shiva Jatra* and similar other festivals. The *Vasudeva Hindi*, a Jain work of the first century A.D., describes a dance held in honour of the lake. It says:

> There was a temple of Arhat Vasupujja there. The eminent persons after paying obeisance to the Arhat, occupied seats at different places under thickets of blooming trees near the lake. At another place near me I noticed a dark complexioned *matangi* girl who looked like a mass of cloud dense just at the time of showers (*jaladāgamasamucchīyā viva megharashi*); with her body decorated with excellent jewellery she looked like a night beautiful with stars.
>
> She was told by her female friends, 'O mistress! you

Religion and Theatre

should be in the service of the great lake by presenting your dance.'

Then she performed her dance like a creeper swaying in the gentle air, clinging on to a blooming Ashoka tree.

Her female friends began singing pleasant songs like female bumble-bees. She produced the splendour of lotus sprouts with the motion of her hands, and with the elegance of a beautiful crane, lifted her leg in succession.

—*WH*, J.C. Jain, p. 155-56.

Rivers, lakes and seas are still worshipped in India with due celebration and rituals. Holy water-resorts are known as *tirthas*. It is interesting to note that their worship includes dance. According to Harivansha, when Yadavas went to *Pindārak Tirtha*, a sea resort near Dwaraka, dances were performed and plays enacted.

The relics of dance-oriented magico-religious rituals still linger in many parts of the country. When a medium or priest is possessed by the spirit of a deity, in his trance he starts dancing in a ferocious manner. Then ensues a dialogue between him and the devotees assembled. The interlocutor utters mysterious answers. This oracle-devotee dialogue was part of the ancient Yaksha worship and was known as *Prashna Vyākarana* or *Brahmōdya*. In the *Mahābhārata* we find an interesting dialogue between Yudhistira and a Yaksha. Many a time, an oracle is a woman, as testified in the ancient Buddhist Sutta literature of 6th century B.C.

Dr. H.K. Ranganath in his work *Karnataka Theatre* makes reference to the *bhūta sthana* or ghost shrines in the coastal villages of Karnataka. He writes:

The impersonator—called Mani—is carefully dressed up in gorgeous costumes mostly made of indigenous vegetation. He is also painted and decorated ... When the impersonator comes into the arena to give 'faith and assurances', he is taken to be directly under the influence of the particular ghost. The dancing party of men called Nalke, all made up in the traditional massive costumes, with *gaggara* tied up to the ankle and swords in hand, dance round 'the ghost' to the vigorous beating of *Tamani*—the traditional drum. Songs of prayer—*pad thane*—are sung in high pitched chorus—all in praise of the particular ghost. The atmosphere will gradually grow in intensity with the faster tempo of the drum-beat and the dance of Mani and Nalke. It is then that Mani will come to be 'possessed' to speak under the spell of the spirit. The whole thing is the creation of unearthly art full of grotesque grandeur and tension.

Dr. H.K. Ranganath remarks that all other folk dances including *Yakshagāna* have taken their basic patterns from the Bhuta dance. Explaining the influence of this ritualistic ghost dance on the majestic *Yakshagāna* theatre of Karnataka, he further states:

> The head-dress called *Battalu Kirita* worn by demons and villains (*prati-nāyaka*) in *Yakshagāna* which seems to have evolved from the head-dress of Mani supports this inference. The indigenous colours traditionally used for the make-up of Mani of *Bhuta Sthana* are also used by the *Yakshagāna* artist for his make-up, and thirdly, the procession of Bhūta and Betāla surrounded by singing Nalkes would give a highly similar picture to that of the court scene in *Yakshagāna*.

It is very interesting to note that Bharata in the second century B.C. was aware of the tradition of *bhūta nritya* or ghost dances. As we have seen earlier he tells us that the performance of *Mahachari*, a ferocious dance (*Raudrapracharanacchapi mahachari—* NS, V. 28), appeases hosts of *Bhutas* Jayasenāpati in his work *Nrityaratnāvali* speaks of *Bhutamātrumahotsava* and acrobatic dances performed on the occasion. He also mentions *vikata nritya* in which a dancer imitates the dress and dances of *Pishāchas* — goblins. It is described as *Vitalam vikrutam nrutyam*. The dancers put on the make-up of goblins and imitate their gaits and fantastic grimaces of parts of the face, of the abdomen, of the arms etc. Probably the sophisticated classical dance styles like *Bharatanatyam*, *Kuchipudi*, and *Odissi* are evolved out of ritualistic dances in honour of the folk deities, as they retain the forceful and acrobatic aspects inherent in the tradition.

The *Teyyam* ritualistic dances are yet another example of the genre. *Teyyam* shrines are found in Kerala and festivals full of ritualistic dances are organised in honour of *Teyyam* deities. Costumes and make-up of dancers impersonating *Teyyam* deities like *Gandharva*, *Yaksha*, *Kuruntuti*, mother-goddess *Puliyirukali*, *Kativanur Veeram* and *Pumarutan* are fantastic and awe-inspiring. Each deity has its own style of dress and make-up with an imposing headdress. The *Teyyam* dancer performs in the temple courtyard. He is then considered as deity itself. He sings songs narrating the stories of the concerned deity, converses with the devotees, listens to their woes, suggests remedies and blesses them. The performance, which starts at midnight, lasts for hours.

The influence of *Teyyam* on Kathakali dance-drama of Kerala is unmistakable.

This goes to show how ritualistic performances finally attain the stature of theatre. The religious scriptures emphatically stressed the significance of theatrical arts as part of rituals to appease deities. For instance the *Agni Purana* states: 'One who offers paintings, music, theatricals, oil, ghee, honey and milk to god, after his death, attains heaven.' The *Yagnavalkya Smriti* says that a person who is well versed in playing on *veena*, knows music and has profound knowledge of rhythm (*tala*) attains salvation without much effort. It further says that *gitagnya*, a person well versed in song and music, after his death enjoys himself by becoming the attendant of Rudra. The *Harivansha Purana* declares that the performer of *Chalikya* dance attains salvation quickly as this form of dance is dear to Lord Narayana. The theatrical arts are considered more important than Yoga as a means of god-realisation. In the *Jaiminyashvamēdhaparva* there is a very interesting dialogue between Krishna and a danseuse. She says:

> O Yogis, see for yourself the Lord who is not won over by your meditation and other rituals is standing before me in person attracted by my dancing. Nothing can please him more, not even the meditation, as the offering of dance, music and songs.

Dhyānēna yōginām naiva lilayā drishyate hari
Sansthitā madbhramēnātra sarvē pashyantu yōgina
Nrutyatām gāyatām chaiva nanāvādya prakurvatām
Yathā santushyatē devō na dhyānādai riti shrutam

Religion and Theatre

The Vaishnava *Bhakti* cult stressed the importance of theatrical arts as a means of salvation—'*mukti*'. In the *Bhagavata Purana* Krishna states that he is immensely pleased by the enactment of his *leelas*, divine acts. The works on dramaturgy also subscribe to this view. Like Bharata, the author of *Nātak Lakshana Ratnakōsha* says: '*Dharmādi sādhanam nātyam*' —the drama is the means or medium to attain *dharma*. *Nātyadarpan* of Ramachandra-Gunabhadra says that drama helps people to achieve *dharma* and *artha*. Poet Kalidasa gives the status of *yajna*, fire sacrifice, to the dramatic performance by calling it *Kratu Chākshusham*. Many authors refer to drama or science of drama as *veda*.

The *Garuda Purāna* enjoins the devotees to build a hall for theatrical performances near the temple. Nata Mandirs or Navaranga Halls for dance, drama and music were attached to temples. Khajuraho group of temples in Madhya Pradesh, Sun Temple at Konarak, Modhera temple in Gujarat, Jagannātha temple at Puri, and Channakeshaveshvara temple at Halebid are some of the temples with beautiful dancing halls. Magnificent theatres called *kūttambalam* were constructed in the premises of Kerala temples for the performance of Sanskrit plays. Temples in Manipur are provided with Nata Mandirs for the enactment of Vaishnava plays. Temples in Gomantak are provided with *Sabhā Mandapas* for the same purpose. The positive attitude of Hindu religious scriptures greatly encouraged the theatre movement in India.

Several inscriptions and copper-plates recording

the endowments to the temples for constructing *Nata Mandapas* and arranging theatricals therein were found all over the country. The custom of dedicating beautiful dancing girls to temples proved beneficial to theatre activities of the religious institutions. Outside *ganikas* and actresses were also invited to perform plays at temples. *Kāmasūtra* of Vātsyāyana enjoins that on festive occasions Samaja—theatrical entertainments—should be held at the temple of Saraswati and actors coming from other places should be rewarded suitably. At Dhar a black stone slab with two acts of the play *Pārijata Manjiri* inscribed on it was recovered from the local Kamal Maula Mosque. The slab was originally a part of a Saraswati temple built by the Parmar kings of Malva. The *Kāmasūtra* says that dramatic festivals should be held in the temples of other deities also. In *Kuttanimatam* we come across a detailed description of the presentation of the play *Ratnāvali* by local *ganikas* in the temple of Kashi Visveshvara. A 10th century inscription of Chitralekha found at Bayana sheds light on various aspects of religion-theatre relationship. It says:

> Good fortune, beauty, kingdom, emancipation and abode in heaven cannot be obtained without worshipping Vishnu. Having thought this ... Chitralekha, the chaste and of esteemed character, caused to be made this temple of Vishnu ... Owing to the temptation of seeing (beautiful temple-girls) them, the enemy of Madhu does not leave his own image for a moment nor does he now remember the heavenly damsels like Rambha and others ... A show given by these ladies whose eyes were like petals of lotus

Religion and Theatre

flowers, whose hips were heavy and whose faces were like the moon was arranged by her (*Ep. Ind.*, Vol. XXII, p. 124).

Building temples, dedicating dancing girls to them and arranging plays for the recreation of the deities was considered meritorious, leading to salvation. It seems that some learned men did try to dissociate theatrical arts from temple worship but strict orders were issued by kings to resist such a move. Jojaldeva's inscription of *Vikram Samvat 1147* clearly states that in no case should the tradition of presenting plays, dance and music performances be discontinued in the temple by his descendants. Otherwise a curse would fall upon them. He says that temple girls should present themselves in their best attire at temple festivals of *Lakshaman Swamin* and other deities with their *shūlapālas*, and they should present dance, music performances. His inscription further states:

> He, who at the time of festival attempts to abolish the practice, be he an ascetic (*tapasvi*), or a learned person (*vidyāwan*), should be prevented from doing so.
> —*Ep. Ind.*, II, p. 26-27

The institution of Devadasis with the passage of time degenerated and went out of practice. But not so the tradition of presenting plays, dance or music performances as an offering to the deities, to appease them. The element of magico-religious ritual is still pronounced in many tribal and folk forms of theatrical arts. Even its echoes are found in the traditional classical dance and dance-drama forms. In the famous Guruvayur temple premises performances of the *Krishnan Attam* cycle of plays are presented before deities in due fulfilment of vows. This dance-drama is still considered a wish-fulfilling ritual. Ram Leela and Krishna Leela plays of India still retain the aura of sacrosanctity and are considered rituals. Ankia Nat plays are performed in the monasteries—*Satra*—of Assam with great devotion. Thus religious lore and mythology dominate the classical dance forms of the country. Despite occasional tensions the relationship between religion and theatre has remained generally cordial in India.

DEVADASI

DEVADASI is a girl dedicated to a temple or a religious establishment to serve its deity in various ways. She can be a high priestess or a consort of the temple's presiding deity, a female oracle or medium of god-communication, participant in magico-religious rituals and performer of theatrical arts, among many other things.

In her ritualistic functions she is connected with the ancient cult of mother-goddesses. In fact since the dawn of civilization woman has been considered a symbol of nature's creative force. In one of the Indus seals a tree is shown sprouting from her. Tree-woman motif, in several alluring varieties and variations, permeates Indian art. It was believed that by her quickening touch trees flower. The Maha Stupa at Sanchi is replete with *Vrikshika* or *Shalbhanjika* sculptures.

She has been an active, many a time a leading participant in magico-religious rituals performed to ensure prosperity and well being of the community. Ritual copulation in the fields, it was believed, enhanced the fertility of the earth. As a symbol of primordial creative energy she is seen associated with religion and ritual though the nature of her participation and contribution differed from time to time.

Vestiges of women's active participation in magico-religious rituals seem to have survived significantly in many religious practices. Many Vedic rituals stand testimony to this. From *Chāndogya* and *Brihadāranyaka Upanishads* it appears that the idea of performing ritual copulation for increasing the fertility of the earth and the belief in magical procreative power of women have influenced many aspects of fire ritual also. Fire is considered as a male principle while the altar containing it is regarded the female principle. The *Chāndogya* says:

> Approaching (the woman with desire) is the syllable 'Him', fascinating (courting, seducing) is the *Prastāva*; sleeping with woman is the *Udgīta*; lying down with the woman is the *Prastāva*; the passing of the time (in love making) is the *Nidhana*; the going to the end (fulfilment) is *Nidhana* (death).
>
> This is the *Vāmadevya* interwoven in the couple. One who thus knows the *Vāmadevya* as interwoven in the couple becomes companioned, goes from coupling to coupling, attains the full span of life, lives gloriously, becomes great in off-spring and cattle, great in fame.
> —II.XIII.1 & 2

The sacrificial fire altar—*Vedi*—is always compared with woman or her procreative organ. *Chāndogya* at yet another place states that

> woman is a sacrificial fire, her procreative organ is fire altar, coital bliss is sparks, gods drop their semen which conceives her (V.1-2).

The *Brihadāranyaka Upanishad* says:

> One who approaches woman with this knowledge acquires

Devadasi 47

the fruits of *Vājapeya Yajna* and also *punya* (VI.4.3).

Shatapatha Brāhmana states:

> The altar should be broader on the west side, contracted in the middle and broad again on the east side; for thus shaped they praise a woman; broad about hips, somewhat narrower between the shoulders and contracted in the middle (or, about waist). Thereby he makes it (the altar) pleasing to the gods (I-2.5.16).

It is significant to note that the dark, mysterious temple-chamber in which the idol is installed is termed as *Garbhagriha* i.e. womb. This is again in recognition of woman's position in religious rituals. Some more evidence can be found in Vedic literature. In the *Ashvamedha Yajna* the chief queen of the sacrifice-performing monarch sleeps under cover with the sacrificed horse. Then starts a dialogue between the *Adhvaryu*, one of the sacrifice-performing priests, and the other queens and maids. Some scholars are of the opinion that initially the priest used to sleep with the chief queen (*Mahishi*). The *Shatapatha Brāhmana* (*Kānd* 13, *Adhyāya* 5, *Brāhmin* 2) gives the details of the ritual in a most frank manner. A ritual animal-woman copulation is sculpted on many temples including those of Modhera and Khajuraho.

The *Mahāvrata* ceremony mentioned in the *Aitareya Āranyaka* is yet another interesting example for understanding woman's position in magico-religious sexual rituals. It is full of music, song, dance, dramatic dialogues and ritual copulation. *Hota* plays on a hundred-stringed *Veena*, girls with pitchers full of water dance round the sacrificial fire, there is a sham fight for an animal hide, striking on the earth-drum, playing on the *Veena* by wives (*Patnyashcha Kandavina*), ritual copulation (*Bhutānāmcha maithunam*) and dialogue between a harlot and a student (*Brahmachāripunschalyohsampravāda*). It is significant to see that woman played a prominent part in the whole procedure. As a temple-girl she later performed many of the functions she had performed in the *Mahāvrata*, including dancing, singing and playing on musical instruments; and in the temple establishments under the influence of *Tantra* cult, even ritual copulation.

In the *Sānkhya* system of philosophy the duality of *Purusha* and *Prakriti* represents the male and female principles in their sublime form. Their union is liberation. *Prakriti* is an active female principle while *Purusha* is the passive participant in her creative activity. A *Sānkhya Kārika* says:

Rangasya darshayitva nivartate yathā nrityan
Purushashya yathātmānam prakashya nivartate prakritih — 59

> (As, after creating a theatrical spectacle danseuse leaves the stage, Prakriti, after exhibiting cosmic activity to Purusha, disappears from the scene.)

A Devadasi acts like and represents a *Prakriti* in the temple ritual, in her dance before the deity.

The most ancient cult of *Tantra*, even pre-vedic in its origin, worships woman and her procreative organ in the symbolic form or even in person. In Vāmāchār rituals the presence and participation of women is a must. In fact *vāmā* means woman and *āchār* is observance, religious, ritualistic or ceremonial. This system propagates five rituals—

> *Madyam māmsam yathā matsyam mudrā maithunamevacha*
> *Shaktipujā vidhāvādye panchatatvam prakīrtitam*
> —*Kulārnava Tantra*

wine, meat, fish, ritual-gestures and copulation. The whole system of dramatic gestures is evolved from ritual-gestures and is again known as *mudra* in dramaturgy. A *Devadasi* in her dance adheres to these *mudras* to appease the deities. In a famous eastern Indian temple she dances nude during god's bed-time signifying divine copulation. She sings erotic songs on the occasion. Devadasis in *Tantrik* establishments, obviously, might have been participating in rituals prescribed by the cult. Abbe J.A. Dubois records a very interesting custom in his work "Hindu Manners, Customs and Ceremonies". He says:

> At Mogur (near Seringapatanam) there is a small temple dedicated to Tipamma, a female divinity, in whose honour a great festival is celebrated every year. The goddess placed in a beautiful palanquin is carried in procession through the streets. In front of her there is another divinity, a male. These two idols, which are entirely nude, are placed in immodest posture and by help of a piece of mechanism a disgusting movement is imparted to them as long as procession continues (Vol II, p. 602-3).

This is obviously a relic of fertility rite. The most visual representation of these rituals is found in the form of Mithuna sculptures—couples in different erotic positions—adorning the walls of Hindu temples. All these rituals recognise the role of women in their execution, hence she is associated with the institution of temples. Many of these rituals have gone out of vogue and, many still exist in a modified form. Accordingly the role of the *Devadasi* also changed.

Shiva and Shakti is yet another sublimated cosmic symbolism representing the male and female procreative principles. In their union originates the universe—*Shiva-Shakti-samayogat jayate srisṭikalpana*. Shiva is represented by *phallus* while Shakti by *yoni*, the female procreative organ. These two combine into a symbol which is worshipped by the devotees of Shiva. It is the Shiva Linga—which is, in fact, linga and yoni combined into one integrated whole, yoni forming the base. This again points at the significant role woman plays in the Shaivite rituals. We have already noted that dancing, singing and love-making form part of Pashupat rituals.

There are two circular *Yogini* temples at Hirapur and Ranipur-Jharial with Shiva shrines in the centre. Yogini-Shiva association again shows the importance of women in the cult. The Hirapur Yoginis are in beautiful dancing attitudes. Girls were consecrated to Shiva temples since ancient times, to perform dances. While describing a *Shiva* temple *Skanda Purana* says that it was resounding with the tinkle of ankle-bells and also bells attached to the girdles of

dancers—*Kanchinūpur shabdena samākirne diganta-
ram.* Shiva Purana enjoins the devotees to dedicate
hundred beautiful girls skilled in dancing and singing
to the Shiva temple—*Uttam stree-sahasraishcha
nrityageyavisharadai.* The cult of Shiva advocated
dancing as part of the rituals.

As we have seen till now, women were very
closely associated with various cultic rituals and this
gave birth to the *Devadasi* system. *Mahābhārata* (in
its *Sabha Parva*) as well as many *Puranas*, while
describing abodes of different deities, wrote about
alluring celestial dancers—*Apsaras*—attached to their
courts. People thought that to make god live in his
image similar recreation should be provided. As we
have earlier seen the *Bayana* inscription says that
owing to the temptation of seeing beautiful temple
girls Vishnu did not leave his image for a moment
and had even forgotten damsels in heaven including
Rambha. Now let us examine the historical evolution
of the *Devadasi* system.

In the *Brahma Jala Sutta*, a Buddhist work of 6th
century B.C., some scholars find a veiled reference to
the *Devadasi* system. The practice of 'obtaining
oracular answers through a girl possessed by the
spirit—*Kumari Panho*' and also of 'obtaining answer
from god—*Deva Panho*' is mentioned by the Buddha
(Sutta 26, verses 15, 16) as low arts. Commenting
on the word *Deva Panho* translator Rhys Davids
remarks: 'Also obtained (oracular answer) through
a girl but this time a Devadasi or temple prostitute.
It is instructive to find even under the patriarchal
regime of the 6th century B.C. that men thought they

could best have communication with gods through the medium of a woman' (Dialogues of Buddha, p. 24). The two terms together point out the association of women with religious establishments and magico-religious rituals. Here her role as a high-priestess or surrogate of the deity, medium of divine communication, is emphasised.

In his encyclopaedic work *Arthashāstra*, written about fourth century B.C., Kautilya refers to Devadasis. In the *Sūtrādhyaksha Prakarana* of the book he states that a Devadasi retired from temple service may be employed in spinning work. Kautilya mentions temple festivals—*Daivata Samājotsava*—full of theatrical entertainments (5.2; 13.5). However he did not define the role of a Devadasi in it. Kautilya mentions another type of religious woman engaged in religious profession termed as *Aditi Stree* (11.1). She earns her livelihood by showing the pictures of different deities to the devotees. But except for mentioning the temple girl he did not say anything more about her. We may, by inference, connect temple festivals with *Devadasis* as the medieval custom suggests. But, Kautilya is silent about her role in temple life.

An interesting fragment of a stone disk depicting a mother goddess in a typical position, her priest, a hut and a girl was found at Rapur. Commenting on it Dr. Devangana Desai in her work *Erotic Sculpture of India* says:

> In the light of James Frazer's theory of the fertile Mother goddess and her priest, the surrogate of the divine bride-

groom, with whom the goddess or her human surrogate, the temple prostitute or Devadasi, mates annually in the cults of fertility for promoting the fruitfulness of earth, corn, mankind, it is possible that the male figure represents the priest or male partner of the goddess. Moreover, a small leaf structure or a 'shrine' is represented on the right of mother goddess. Could it be the earliest pictorial representation of the shrine in India? On the right side of the 'shrine' there is another male figure who offers a round object to a fully clad female. Her hair is arranged in one plait. Can it be presumed that she was the human surrogate of the Mother goddess, i.e., a Devadasi or a prototype of a Devadasi? (p. 11, plate 1)

However a steatite plaque with three panels found at Rajgir, belonging to 2nd century B.C. (given in her book as plate 2) reflects the *Devadasi* concept more clearly. In one panel a Devadasi is posing as a deity with a priest standing before her. In the second panel a priest is offering her a cup, probably of wine, and in the third panel a Devadasi is seen dancing while the priest is shown playing on the elongated drum—*Mridanga*. Dancing and music as part of rituals used to be offered to the deity and the tradition is still in vogue. Devadasi might be dancing after being possessed by the divinity, as her human surrogate. Here we get an important evidence of one of the major tasks of *Devadasis*, i.e., dancing before the deity.

One of the earliest inscriptions mentioning a Devadasi by name is located in the Jogimara cave in Madhya Pradesh. The transcription and translation of the five line inscription by T. Bloch reads as follows:

Sutanuka nāma
devadāsikyi
Sutanuka nama ı devadasikyi ı
tam kamayitha bal(a)naseye ı
devadine nama ı lupadakhe ı

(Sutanuka by name,
a Devadasi.
Sutanuka by name, a devadasi.
The excellent among young men love her,
Devadinna by name, skilled in sculpture.)
—ASIR, 1903-4, Critique of Indian Theatre, p. 95-107

The Sitabenga cave is considered as a cave theatre of 3rd century B.C. The inscription in this cave suggests that there 'poetry was recited, love songs were sung and theatrical performances acted, particularly at the 'swing-festival' of the vernal full moon, when frolics and music abound.' Participation of Sutanuka in it was inevitable. It is evident from literary evidence that caves were used as pleasure resorts in ancient India. If we believe Prof. Luders' explanation of the term *lenashobhika* (which occurs in the Mathura inscription) as cave actresses we may conclude that there was a class of performers who used to entertain people at cave resorts. *Chullavagga* tells us about the *giragga samagga*—a festival at the mountain top which was full of dancing, singing and music—at Rajagaha. Was Sutanuka a cave actress dedicated to the cave temple at Ramgarh hill?

These inscriptions give us further information about *Devadasis*. They used to entertain people assembled on festive occasions at temples in nearby theatre halls (later in *Nata Mandirs*) and these brides of god were available to people like Devadinna who was a banker, actor, sculptor or painter. Many scholars consider him as a banker of Banaras. Entertaining deities and the devotees became their job.

As we have earlier seen many panels sculpted on the railings or gateways of Stupas at Bharhut, Sanchi and Amaravati show worship being offered to the relic of Buddha or to his headdress or to the Bodhi-tree. Dancing, singing and music by charming girls was part of the worship. On the Prasenjit pillar of the Bharhut stupa a musical opera performed by four Apsaras—*Alambusa*, *Misakesi*, *Padumavati* and *Subhada* is depicted beautifully. We do not know if these dancing and singing girls belonged to Buddhist establishments. Most probably they were invited to present dances on festive occasions or at the time of worship. There was a class of professional *Ganikas* who used to perform at religious establishments without belonging to them.

For instance in the *Meghaduta* of poet Kalidasa there occurs a beautiful description of spectacular evening worship at the Mahākal Temple of Ujjain. The atmosphere was filled with the tinkle of the girdle-bells worn by the dancing girls. They were fanning the idol with whisk and feeling tired by the exercise. Kalidasa says:

> O Cloud, when the rain drops will fall on the nail-marks on their bodies due to last night's love-making they will cast happy glances at you.

Here Kalidasa uses the words *'Leelavadhu'* and *'Veshya'* meaning pleasure-women and prostitutes and not the term *Devadasi*. It appears that some pleasure-women were employed as part-time *Devadasis* in the Mahakal temple.

As we have earlier seen, in the one act play *Ubhayābhisārika* of Vararuchi, belonging to early Gupta period, there is a mention of a *Ganika*, Madanasena, being invited to the temple of Bhagavan Narayan to present a Sangeetak—musical opera—named *Madanārādhana*. She was a prostitute by profession and not a Devadasi. The eleventh century work *Kathā-Sarit-Sāgara* mentions a beautiful and young prostitute of Mathura named Rupanika who used to visit a local temple at the time of worship to perform her appointed duty (2.4.78-80). She was a *Vāravilasini* performing duties of a *Devadasi*.

Another interesting example is found in the eighth century work of poet Damodargupta entitled *Kuttanimatam*. Once prince Samarbhatta of Devarāshtra (ancient Mahārāshtra) visited the Vishvanātha temple at Kāshi. After the worship he was surrounded by dancers, flute-players, singers and prostitutes and also rich traders. This shows that entertainers were always flocking the temples with the hope of earning something from the rich pilgrims. The dance-master would ask the prince if he would like to watch *Sangeet*—a musical play. He would then present before him a *Ganika* named Manjiri and her friends who would enact the first act of the play *Ratnāvali* of Shriharsha. These girls were not Devadasis, but seem to have been working as temple entertainers.

However the Nrityāchārya is not happy about these common prostitutes. He sadly says:

> One cannot expect excellence in dramatic performance at a place where knave *Dasis* act in the play as characters. Even after appearing on stage these women do not hesitate to leave it on hearing about the arrival of some known person at their homes. *Veshyas* who indulge in drinking and meat-eating, and who lust after men, cannot show excellence in acting. Without any enthusiasm they sometimes do move their hands and legs in the name of acting due to the fear of losing their means of livelihood.

Despite this tirade from a dance-master, Manjiri seems to have perfect mastery over the art of acting and dancing. These girls were invited to perform at a temple to which no permanent band of *Devadasis* was attached. However in verse 742, poet Damodar refers to a *Devadasi* attached to the *Gambhīrēshvar* temple, which still stands at Scindia Ghat at Kāshi.

In the *Kāmasutra* of Vātsyāyana written in the early centuries of Christian era, citizens are advised to hold *Samāja* at the temple of Saraswati and other deities and invite local or outside dramatic troupes to perform plays. Vātsyāyana did not mention about *Devadasis*.

The *Rājatarangini*, a historical chronicle written by Kalhana, gives us interesting information about the *Devadasi* system. In the fourth *taranga* occurs a story of eighth century king Jayapida who was 'versed in the histrionic arts of the dance, song and the like in accordance with Bharata's *Nātyashāstra*'. In the city of Paundravardhana in the Gauda he visited a temple of Kārtikeya to witness a dance accompanied by vocal and instrumental music. A danseuse named Kamala was enamoured by his beauty and took him home. This points out the tradition of temple prostitution. We have already referred to the story of two mysterious dancers and the excavation that resulted in the discovery of temples of Keshava. A pious king named Jalauka (2nd century B.C.) dedicated hundreds of ladies of the royal household who had got up to dance at the hour of dancing and singing (1.151). When king Durlabhaka Pratāpāditya II fell in love with a merchant's wife named Srinarendraprabha, the husband proposed to the king that he will dedicate his wife to the temple as a danseuse on account of her knowledge of dancing and that from there he (the king) could take her to the royal harem (4.36). This seems to be the custom of the land. Girls were offered to kings through temples. *Devadasis* were interested in the affairs of the state. Among the class of people who 'take delight in the upheavals against the king', 'the superannuated dancing women of the temples of the gods' are enumerated (8.706-10). King Utkarsha's (early 11th century A.D.) mistress Sahaja was formerly 'a resident dancing girl of a temple, who having been seen on the stage, had been taken into the seclusion of the palace as the consort of the king (VII.858).' She committed Sati on the death of her young royal lover. Though she was liked and loved by the next king Harsha she embraced death. *Rajatarangini* says:

> While she was courtesan, she had at one time been the

sweetheart of Harshadeva also and hence he had besought her, yet she did not desist from death.

This shows yet another aspect of the character of *Devadasis*.

There are many instances of beautiful courtesans and temple girls becoming queens or being taken to the royal harem as mistresses. *Rajatarangini* records the story of the king Uccala of early 12th century who married a girl from a dancing family called Jayamati (VII.1460-1462). We find the earliest mention of the *Devadasi* system in Assam in the Tezpur grant of Vanamala from which we learn that girls were dedicated to a temple of Shiva. The 18th century king Shiva Singh married a beautiful *Nat*, temple dancing girl, of a Shiva temple whose name was Phuleshvari. *Nat Kalita* community of artists provides dancers to temples in Assam. *Natis* are called Devadasis. Haijo temple of Hayagriva Mādhava was a great centre of Devadasis since ancient times. The Devadasis of famous Kamākhya temple at Gauhati are known as Deodhani. They perform frenzied dances in the Nata Mandir of the temple as if possessed by the deity. These god women and their consorts—*Deodhan*—are associated with the worship of the serpent goddess Manasa.

In fact Puranas contributed significantly to the evolution and development of the Devadasi system in India. They stressed temple festivity and exhibition of theatrical arts by Devadasis dedicated to the temple. *Agni Purana* enjoins the devotees to arrange *Jatras* (*Yātrā devasya kārayet*) in honour of deities, full of dancing, singing and sounding of musical instruments (*Gitanrityādivādyakaih*). Consecration of a deity is left unrewarded if a grand festival is not organised on the occasion (*Utsavēnavinā yasmāsthapana nishphalam bhavet*). It further says that the person offering paintings, dancing, singing, dramatic performances attains heaven after death (*Chitrakrudwitavādyadiprēkshanıyadidānakrita...devam divam vrajet*).

In the *Srishti Khānda* of *Padma Purāna* devotees are enjoined to dedicate beautiful girls to Muni and to the temple. It says:

Muninām prēyasī narī yuvatī rūpashālinīm
Sālamkārām sashayyāncha datvānantaphalam labhet
Kritā devāya dātavya dheerena klishta karmanā
Kalpakalē bhavēt swarga nrupo vasau mahadhanī
—52.97-100

On the profusely carved plinth of Kandariya Mahadeva temple at Khajuraho there is an interesting sculpture showing a pot-bellied priest sitting comfortably and a Devadasi dancing before him. This illustrates the first two lines of the above mentioned quotation. It further says that a person who dedicates girls to deities attains heaven.

There are many references to the Devadasi system in the *Skanda Purāna*. King Vajrāngadeva, it says, dedicated dancing girls to serve god Shonanātha (24.12). *Bhavishya Purana* states:

Vēshyakadambakam yastu dadyātsūryāya bhaktitah

Devadasi

> Sa gacchet paramam sthānam yatra tishthati
> Bhānuman
>
> —93.67

If dancing girls are dedicated to the Sun god after death the person attains *Surya Loka* or the abode of Sun god. Hieun Tsang who visited India in the 7th century speaks of dancing girls at the Sun temple of Multan. Same was the condition of the Sun temple at Konarak where Madana Mahotsavas used to be performed full of theatrical entertainments. On the plinth and pillars of Nata Mandapa, dancing hall, of this temple there is a profusion of dancing figures in different poses and also of jesters. We have earlier noted the Bayana inscription of Chitralekha which speaks of beautiful dancing girls presenting plays — *Prēksha*—before the idol of Vishnu. Also we have seen the inscription which records the grant for arranging theatricals in the Krishna temple in Rajasthan.

It is evident from the ancient mariner's manual of the coasts of India entitled *Periplus of the Erythrean Sea* that along with wine, beautiful Yavana dancing girls were imported to India for royal harems. Some of them seem to have found their way into the local flesh market and some, it seems, were even dedicated to temples as Devadasis. In the *Bhana Padatadikam*, written by Mahākavi Shyamalik in the early 5th century, there occurs a beautiful description of a Yavana courtesan settled in the prosperous city of Ujjain. Her name is given as Karpoorturishtha. In the year 1899 during the excavation in Egypt undertaken by the Biblical Archaeological Association a Greek farce with Kannada passages was found. It was dated 2nd century A.D. It seems that the heroine of the farce, a beautiful Greek girl called Charition, was dedicated to the temple of the moon-goddess situated near Malpe in Karnataka. The buffoon who came along with the party of rescuers advised her to steal some of the valuable offerings made to the goddess but she refuses to do so. The following conversation ensues between them:

> Buffoon : Lady Charition, get ready, if you can take under your arm one of the offerings to the goddess.
> Charition : Hush! Those in need of salvation must not accompany their petitions to the gods with sacrilege. For how will they listen to the prayers of those who are about to gain mercy by wickedness? The property of a goddess must remain sacred.
> Buffoon : Don't you touch it; I will carry it.
> Charition : Don't be silly.
> —Ancient Indian & Indo-Greek Theatre, p. 99-103

This is a very touching example of the deep devotion of a Devadasi towards the temple deity.

Sacred prostitution in one form or the other was prevalent in the ancient world. It was a universal phenomenon. The code of *Hammurabi* and the epic of *Gilgamesh*, ascribed to *c.* 2000 B.C., mention temple girls. In Greece girls were dedicated to temples, particularly of Aphrodite. Xenophon of Corinth dedicated 25 girls to Aphrodite on winning two events in Olympic games in the year 464 B.C. Pindar wrote a beautiful poem describing the charm of the girls. While describing the temple of Bel, the Babylonian Zeus, the great historian Herodotus says:

> The shrine contains no image and no one spends the night there except (if we may believe the Chaldeans who are the priests of Bel) one Assyrian woman, all alone, whoever it may be that the god has chosen. The Chaldeans also say—though I do not believe them—that the god enters the temple in person and takes his rest upon the bed. There is a similar story told by the Egyptians at Thebes, where a woman always passes the night in the temple of the Theban Zeus and is forbidden, like the woman in the temple at Babylon, to have intercourse with men; and there is yet another instance in the Lycian town of Patara, where the priestess who delivers the oracles when required is shut up in the temple during the night.

He further states:

> There is one custom among these people which is wholly shameful: every woman who is a native of the country must once in her life go and sit in the temple of Aphrodite and there give herself to a strange man.

The most interesting inscription indicating the magnitude of Devadasi system is that of Rājarāja Chola, builder of Brihadeshvara temple at Tanjore. The inscription mentions by name some four hundred dancing girls brought from various Shaiva and some Vaishnava temples in his territory. The scholars have identified many of these temples in the Tamil land. The inscription also mentions a host of temple staff including dance-masters, musicians, drummers, singers etc. In the premises of this magnificent temple stands a circular Kuravanji platform – an open-air stage—for dancers to perform. It is said that the temple dancers used to enact *Rājarāja Nātakam*, depicting the history of temple construction (South Indian Inscriptions, Vol. 2, Part III, p. 259). Nearly every South Indian temple of significance had Devadasis who used to dance before the deities, perform plays and perform many kinds of temple duties entrusted to them by the temple administration.

Rājarāja Chola provided for the living of Devadasis – *tali-cheri-pendugal* – and other performing artistes attached to the great temple. They were given land grants, houses, and sometimes a share in the temple income. K. Satyanarayana in his work *A Study of History and Culture of Andhra*, referring to the Kopparam grant (Narsaraopet taluk) dated 1115 A.D., says:

> We find that the temple trustee was given 10 khandikas of wet land and 5 of dry one; the priest got 2 khandikas of wet land and 5 of dry one; the dancing-master received 4 khandikas of wet and 6 khandikas of dry land, while the dancing mistress got 6 and 12; the dancing girl received 3 and 5 khandikas and the female musician another 3 and 5; the flute player got 3 and 5 khandikas.
> —SII, VI, No. 74; Epi Glossary of Andhra Pradesh, Hyderabad, 1967

In Karnataka many inscriptions between 11th to 13th centuries speak of grants on account of

1. Protima Bedi on the background of wheel of Sun Temple, Konarak

2. Ritual Dance, Bhimbetka Cave, Madhya Pradesh

3. Worship of Bodhi Tree with song, dance and music, Sanchi

4. Musician at Buddhist Temple, Airtam, Uzbekistan

5. Buddhist Lama Dances, Bhutan

6. Bhuta (Ghost) Dance, Karnataka

7. Theyyam, Kerala

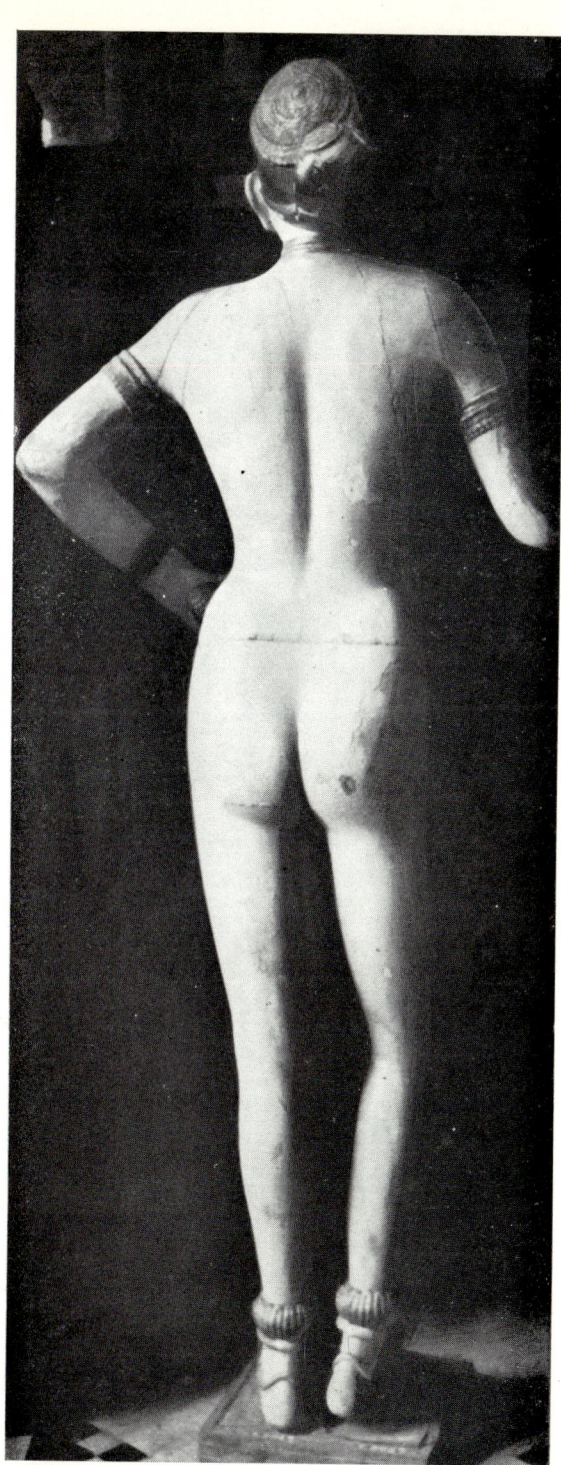

8. Devadasi, wood sculpture from Orissa, Ashutosh Museum

9. Stone Disk showing Devadasi, priest, temple and goddess, Rupar

10. Devadasi and priest, steatite plaque, Rajgir →

11. Ritual copulation in yogic posture, Khajuraho

12. Prakriti and Purush, Konarak

13. Brihadeshvar Temple, Tanjor
15. Devadasi dance, Hajo Temple, Assam

14. Mahari—temple dancer, Jagannatha Temple, Puri

16. Swapna Sundari, Dance Festival, Khajuraho

Rangabhōga which may mean patronage to stage, or performance of drama or religious dialogues. Temples employed singers, dancing-masters, dancing girls and a stage manager (*Karnataka Through the Ages*). Beautiful *Navaranga* halls with circular dancing-arena connected with the *Garbhagriha* by *shukanasi* is the special feature of Hoyasala temples of the period.

Pillalmarri inscription of Receruvula Nami Reddi records the gift of about nineteen houses to the temple dancers. It says:

> The glorious Receruvula Nami Reddi gave away, after pouring water, the following houses (list given) in the front of Pillalmarri for those who gave public enjoyment (entertainment) to the Lord of the temple of the glorious Nameshvara.
>
> —Hyderabad Archaeological Series, No. 13, 1942, p. 109

An inscription found at Vaghli near Chalisgaon in Khandesh, Maharashtra belonging to 1069 A.D. records the gift of four acres of land to the temple of Siddheshvara Shiva by *Maurya-Kula-Pradīpa* prince Gōvindrāja. It also shows the magnitude of temple activity and its position in the social structure as a centre of art, culture and learning. It says:

> *Gōvindarājōpi dadau grā(ma)yo(rma)ntha (bhō)-gakam*
> *Mēlakā devapujārtha ghrānak dīpasiddaye*
> *Pātākam gītanrityārtha vilāsinīsamanvitā*
> *Trushkalam devabhōgārtha gachakānām cha bhūmi*
> *Viprānām bhōjanārthāyam sātra(cha) muddishnā shasvatam*

*Vidyābhyāsaratānāmcha chātra(cha)na bhōjanā-
yacha
Kshētrāni yāni bhūpalo dadau tāni likhābhyatah*
—*Ep. Ind.,* Vol. II, p. 227

The grant is for covering the expenditure on ritual worship, dance performances by prostitutes, food and shelter for students and Brahmins etc. Dr. M. Rama Rao in his book *Select Kakatiya Temples* tells us how the income from various taxes was donated to temples for the maintenance of temple girls etc. He says:

> Ambadeva, the famous Kakatiya chief remitted at the instance of the teacher taxes from the villages of the temples for the purpose of supplying perfumes and clothes for the use of gods, for employing musicians and dancers and for constructing a choultry for feeding the Brahmins, ascetics, Vīra-vratas, Māheshvaras, Pāshupatas, Kālmukhas, Bhairavas and Yamalas that visited Tripurāntakam (p. 44).

We find evidence to show that some Devadasis made generous grants to the religious establishments. We have already seen the inscription of Lenashobhika of Mathura who had erected a shrine to Arhat, a hall of homage and a cistern. At the famous Virupaksha temple of Pattadakal an inscription of the time of Rastrakuta Dhruva is found. It records the gift given to the temple by a Devadasi of queen Loka-Mahadevi's temple. Her name is given as Badi-poddi daughter of Goyinda-poddi. A Nata Mandir— dancing hall—at the famous Suchindrum temple in

Tamil Nadu was built by the donations given by the temple Devadasis. It was used for staging *Shiva Leela* plays.

The foreign visitors have left behind a very interesting account of the Devadasi system in India. Al-Baruni, a historian and a savant who had accompanied Mahmud of Gazni at the time of sack of famous Somanath temple in the year 1025 A.D., narrates the splendour of this religious establishment. He says that there were about three hundred dancing girls attached to the temple who used to dance before Lord Somanath in the morning and evening. Scholars like Dr. Harkant Shukla feel that they were probably dedicated to the temple by the South Indian rulers.

The famous Venetian traveller and explorer Marco Polo (1256-1323 A.D.) who travelled through India and visited Malabar at the end of the 13th century in his records made interesting observations about the local system of temple dancers. He says:

> They have certain abbeys in which are gods and goddesses to whom many young girls are consecrated, their fathers and mothers presenting them to that idol for which they entertain the greatest devotion.
> And when the (monks) of the convent desire to make a feast to their god they send for all those consecrated damsels and make them sing and dance before the idol with great festivity.
> They also bring meats to feed their idol withal; that is to say, the damsels prepare dishes of meat and leave it there a good while, and then the damsels all go to their dancing and singing and festivity for about as long as a great Baron might require to eat his dinner. By that time

they say the spirit of the idols has consumed the substance of the food, so they remove the viands to be eaten by themselves with great jollity. This is performed by these damsels several times every year until they are married.

The reason assigned for summoning the damsels to these feasts is, as the monks say, that the god is vexed and angry with the goddess, and will hold no communication with her; and they say that if peace be not established between them the things will go from bad to worse, and they never will bestow their grace and benediction. So they make these girls come in the way described, to dance and sing, all but naked, before the god and goddess. And those people believe that the god often solaces himself with the society of the goddess.

—The Book of Ser Marco Polo, Vol. II, p. 345-46 (Ed. 1975), Yule & Cordier

The great empire of Vijayanagar was founded by Harihara and Bukka in the mid-14 century which reached the peak of its glory under the rule of Krishnadevaraya. During the time Domingos Paes visited the empire and in his chronicle included the information about the Devadasi system. He says:

These pagodas (temples) are buildings in which they pray and have their idols; the idols are of many sorts, namely figures of men and women, of bulls and apes, while others have nothing but round stone (Shiva Linga?) which they worship. In this temple of Darcha is an idol with the figure of a man for its body, and the face of an elephant with trunk and tusks (Ganapati), and with three arms on each side and six hands, of which arms they say that already four are gone, and when all fall then the world will be destroyed; they are full of belief that this will be, and hold it as a prophecy.

They feed the idol every day,' for they say that he eats;

and when he eats women dance before him who belong to that pagoda, and they give him food and all that is necessary, and all girls born of these women are of loose character, and live in the best streets that there are in the city; it is the same in all their cities, their streets have the best rows of houses.

They are very much esteemed and are classed amongst those honoured ones who are the mistresses of the captains; any respectable man may go to their houses without any blame attaching thereto. These women (are allowed) even to enter the presence of the wives of the king, and they stay with them and eat betel with them, a thing which no other person may do, no matter what his rank may be.

—Vijayanagar Empire, Paes and Nuniz, p. 24

This speaks of the high social rank enjoyed by the Devadasis in Vijayanagar empire, and, also, of their prosperity. Around many temples in India houses were allotted to *Devadasis*. Abdur Razak who visited Vijayanagar also had an occasion to witness a dance performance before the idol during Mahanavami festival. Enchanted by the superb skill of the dancers he says:

> The girls began to move their feet with such grace that wisdom lost its head and soul was intoxicated with delight.
>
> —Elliot: History of India, IV, p. 118

A play Jāmbavatī Kalyāṇam on the Krishna theme was written by Krishnadevaraya. On the occasion of Chaitra festival of Virūpāksha of Vijayanagar it was enacted. Probably *Devadasis* attached to the temple might have participated in the play.

Plays were enacted by temple girls all over India. We have already noted that in the Bayana inscription of Chitralekha the *Prēkshas* were staged in temple. In the fifth canto of the *Antya Khanda* of *Shri Chaitanya Charitāmrita* by Shrikrishnadas Goswami there is a detailed description of how Rāmānanda Rai trained the Devadasis of Puri temple to act in his play *Jagannātha Vallabha*. He used to bathe and massage two young *Deva Kanyas* whom he kept in his house and also do their make-up with his own hands. He taught them how to dance, delineate the meaning of the song through acting, how to express emotions, and basic sentiments through eyes, facial and bodily movements.

The earliest mention of Devadasi in Orissa is found in the 10th century inscription of king Udyot Kesari, which records the construction of the Brahmēshvar temple. The lyrical temple inscriptions speak of the delightful beauty of temple girls locally known as *Maharis*. If the sculptures of the enchanting *Surasundaris* adorning Orissan temples are any indication of the beautiful girls dedicated to the temples the descriptions of the inscriptions are not far from truth. For instance, the above mentioned inscription says:

> By her (Queen-Mother Kolavati) were dedicated to god Shiva some beautiful women, whose limbs were adorned with ornaments set in gems and thus appearing as the everlasting but playful lightnings.

The twelfth century Mēghēshvar temple inscription,

Devadasi

now attached to Ananta Vasudeva temple at Bhuvaneshvar, says:

> Their eye-lashes constitute the very essence of captivating the whole world; when they are walking or dancing, all the three worlds, ceasing their activities, start looking at them in wonder—*Padanyāsa tribhuvanagati stambhanam.*

Even beautiful queens and princesses took pride in dancing before the deities in the temple. Queen Shantala who is described in an inscription (EC, Vol. V, BI 58) as 'a jewelled lamp in the house of *Bharatāgama* (*Nātyashāstra*), a hand-jewel in all manners of dancing and Saraswati in singing', used to dance in the Channakēshaveshvara temple at Belur as well as Jain and Shiva temples at Halebid built by her husband Vishnuvardhana of 12th century A.D.

Jagannatha temple at Puri became a great cultural centre where fine arts flourished over centuries. Temple girls took important part in theatrical activities. They used to dance at various *Yatra* processions of deities with great devotion. The tradition of staging Jayadeva's *Geeta Gōvinda* was kept alive by them. There is an interesting series of panels in the compound of the Bhuvaneshvar museum showing *Ratha Yatra* in progress. Temple dancing girls are seen prominently in the procession. A code of conduct prescribed for the *Maharis* defines their role in the temple set up. A high standard of morality is also stressed. Pandit Sadashiva Ratha Sharma of Puri gives the extract from a royal decree found in the possession of an old *Mahari* named Buli. It says:

The order prohibits the *Maharis* from having physical contact with men. They should not dance in any festival except those of Lord Jagannatha. After initiation in Vaishnavism they should adorn their body with the marks of Tilak and Kali. They should not take food cooked at home nor should they speak to any male on the days they are to dance before the Lord.

They should wear clean clothes. They should be led to the temple by *Mina Nayak* on the occasion of the performance. While dancing they should not look at the pilgrim audience. They should dance according to directions of the *Shastra* and think of themselves as servants of god. The dancer and singer should progress in perfect cooperation. There should not be any flaw in *Tala* and *Swara* (rhythm and melody). They should dance on the following *Talas—Pahapata, Sariman, Parameshvar Malasree, Herachandi, Malashri, Chandana Jhula, Srimangala Bachanika, Jhuti Ath Tali* and should make *Abhinaya* of the songs from the *Geeta Govinda*.

However the *Devadasi* system degenerated fast and all sort of immoralities set in. The brides of god became concubines of priests, feudal lords and kings. Some of them amassed huge wealth and stopped serving temples. Faith in old values dwindled. Not much difference remained between the common prostitutes and the temple girls. A Persian work *Sirat-i-Firuz Sahi* which relates the story of Feroz Shah Tughlak's attack on Puri in 1361 A.D. says:

> Bevies of daughters of the Rais and Brahmins, misguided and seduced, throng here from distant parts and places; troops of the followers of the female devil sanyasis who are called *masavasi*, and garrulous persons who are called *Bhurja* squat on the ground and lead the people astray.
> —JRASB, Vol. VIII, 1942, p. 74

Devadasi 73

Sir William Hunter is equally critical of the Devadasi system. However some of his observations are hard to believe, particularly those connected with the Janmashtami festival at Puri temple. He says:

> Indecent ceremonies disgraced the ritual, and dancing girls with rolling eyes made the modest female worshippers blush . . . The baser feature of the worship which aims at a sensuous realisation of God appears in a band of prostitutes who sing before God's image . . . In the pillared hall a choir of dancing girls enliven the idols' repast by their airy gyrations . . . The indecent rites which have crept into Vaishnavism, and which, according to the spirit of the worshipper, are either highly mystical or mere obscenities, are best represented by the birth festival (Janmashtami) in which a priest takes a part of a father and a dancing girl that of a mother of Jagannatha and the ceremony of this nativity is performed true to life.
> —A History of Orissa, Vol. I, p. 35, 36; Bengal Dist. Gazetteer, 1908, quoted by D.N. Patnaik

The Janmashtami ritual, if true, represents the cult of magico-religious copulation to ensure fertility which we find in the Mahāvrata ceremony of Vedic times. However in the ultimate analysis it seems that the original role of the *Devadasi* changed a lot and she mainly became a temple entertainer in later times, though, she may have retained some of the features of the old tradition.

At the end of 18th century Abbe J.A. Dubois worked in south India and recorded his impressions of Hindu society. His French manuscript was translated by H.K. Beauchamp under the title *Hindu*

Manners, Customs and Ceremonies in two volumes. Talking about the *Devadasi* system he says:

> The courtesans or dancing girls attached to each temple take their part in the second rank; they are called *Devadasis* but the public call them by the more vulgar name of prostitutes. In fact they are bound by their profession to grant their favours, if such they be, to anybody demanding them in return for ready money.
>
> Every temple of any importance has in its service a band of eight, twelve or more. Their official duties consist in dancing and singing within a temple twice a day, morning and evening, and also at the public ceremonies. The first they execute with sufficient grace, although their attitudes are lascivious and their gestures indecorous. As regards their singing, it is always almost confined to obscene verses describing some licentious episode in the history of their god.
>
> They employ all the sources and artifices of coquetry. Perfumes, elegant costumes, coiffures best suited to set off the beauty of their hair, which they entwine with sweet-scented flowers, a profusion of jewels worn with much taste on different parts of the body; graceful and voluptuous attitudes—such are the snares with which these sirens allure the Hindus.
>
> The dancing women, the chorus and the orchestra take turns during the religious ceremony which often terminates with a procession about temple.
>
> —1897 Edition, p. 592-5

Though the names by which *Devadasis* were called, the mode of their offering to deities and their relationship with temple administration differed from region to region in the country, their basic duties remained practically the same. Initially the stress was more on their role as partners in magico-religious rituals and since medieval period they became temple entertainers and custodians of fine arts. They contributed significantly to the evolution and development of music, dance and drama and thus preserved the tradition of Bharata's *Nātyashāstra*. The temple thus became the cultural centre of the community. Various styles of classical dance evolved by *Devadasis* like *Dasi Natyam*, *Odissi* and *Kathak* are now widely performed by present day dancers.

It was not that everything was smooth-sailing for the *Devadasi* system during the long course of its history. Muslim rule posed a great threat to their existence, particularly in north India. From the temples Kathak dancers went to courts and *Kothas*. Religious *Rās* theatre which emerged in Vraj region was required to recruit child actors. It seems that there was a great opposition to the degenerated form of this system from Brahmins and sages. As we have seen earlier, king Jojaldeva was required to issue a decree in the form of an inscription prohibiting any efforts to put an end to the *Devadasi* system, whether it be made by a *Vidyawan* (learned person) or a *Tapasvi* (an ascetic). He pronounced a curse on all those who would work in this direction.

However Brahmins did revolt against the *Devadasi* system, particularly in Andhra Pradesh. In this region the *Devadasis* were attached to Shiva temples in particular and they used to dance on the stone slab — *Balipida*—placed behind the *Nandi*, sacred bull of the deity. A temple at Palampet is adorned with exquisite sculptures of temple dancers in various attitudes as per the science of dance—*Nrittaratnāvali*—written by Jayasenapati. Brahmins well versed in dramaturgy believed that the association of Devadasis with religious theatre was sacrilegious. They assembled at a village Kuchipudi and started the tradition of Brahman Melas, a dramatic form based on the tenets of Bharata, and kept *Devadasis* out. It spread to different parts of south India assuming different local names; for instance it became *Bhāgavata Mela* on reaching Tanjore and *Melattur* in Tamil Nadu. Many theatrical forms like *Yakshagāna*, *Kathakali* and even *Krishnan Attam* which were directly connected with the temple institution did not find women in them due to different reasons. In the Vaishnava monasteries of Assam (*Satra*), founded by Mahāpurusha Shankaradeva, good-looking celibate monks acted the roles of women in *Ankia Nat* plays, though *Devadasis* continued to dance in *Shaiva* and *Vaishnava* temples in the region.

THEATRE OF BHAGAVATAS

IN his historical chronicle *Rājatarangini* (River of Kings) poet Kalhana of Kashmir records an interesting episode about king Lalitaditya Muktapida who came to the throne at the end of the 7th century A.D. He states:

> On one occasion that king, who was an expert in horsemanship, took into the jungle all alone an untrained horse in order to train it himself.
>
> In that place which was remote from human habitation, he saw from a distance one maiden with a lovely figure who was singing and another who was dancing.
>
> While he was training the horse he saw that after a while, having concluded the song and the dance, the two doe-eyed maidens after bowing slightly were going away.
>
> Mounting the horse he came to the place day after day and seeing those two lovely girls in the same attitude he went and asked them in astonishment.
>
> To him the two of them said, 'We are dancing girls belonging to a temple; yonder is the village Suravardhamana, our house is there. Upon the spiritual instruction of our mothers, who used to obtain living at this place, by our family the dancing has been ceremoniously carried on here. This custom has been handed down one generation to another and been established in our house; neither of us nor any one else knows the reason for this.'
>
> After hearing the statement of those two girls, the king was amazed and the following day, he had the entire terrain excavated by labourers.
>
> When they had removed the earth far down, the king,

as reported by them, saw a couple of ancient temples the doors of which were closed. When the door-panels were opened, he there saw two images of Keshava.

—Tr. Pandit, IV, 265-274

This historical account clearly establishes the close relationship of the ancient cult of *Bhagavatas*, based on the worship of Vasudeva-Krishna, to theatrical arts. Dance, music and drama formed part of Bhagavata rituals and worship since ancient times. As we have seen earlier the grammarian Patanjali refers to musical ensembles performing at the temple of Keshava—*mṛdaṅgasaṅkha tūnavah pṛthannadanti samsadi prasāde Dhanapati-Rama-Keshavanam*. He also mentions the performance of the plays *Kansa Vadha* and *Bali Vadha* based on *Bhāgavata* themes.

The Bhāgavata cult which was adorned by ancient Greeks also has Vasudeva-Krishna as its supreme deity. He is called *Natavar*, the supreme actor, in the *Bhāgavata Purana*. The first known dramatist of India is Bhāsa who wrote eight plays around 400 B.C. The *Nāndi Shlokas* (opening prayer songs) of a majority of his plays are dedicated to Krishna and his incarnations. He has written two interesting Krishna plays—*Bālacharitam* and *Dūtavākyam*. His writings betray deep influence of the *Bhāgavata* cult. He calls Krishna a Sūtradhāra—the string-holder of the universal drama of life.

Lokatrayavirātanātaktantravastu-
Prastāvanāpratisamāpana Sūtradhārah
—Dūtaghatōtkacha

Theatre of Bhagavatas

All the three worlds—*Swarga*, *Mrutyu*, *Pātāla*—constitute a stage on which the eternal drama of life is going on. As the *Sūtradhāra* or the director controls the entire play, Nārāyana-Krishna is managing this grand spectacle from its beginning to its grand finale. Bhasa is the first dramatist to present *Hallisaka-Rās* dance associated with the *Bhāgavata* cult, on the stage. This again shows the influence of the cult on early Indian theatre.

The Bhāgavata cult seems to have influenced *Nātyashāstra* of Bharata written around 2nd century B.C. Enumerating ten kinds of drama Bharata says that their basic source is *Vritti—Sarvēshāmēva kāvyānām mātrukā vrittayah smrutāh* (20.4). In the 22nd chapter he says that *Vrittis* emanated from Vishnu-Krishna. Hence Hari is the source of dramatic arts. Adya Rangacharya has explained *Vrittis* as singing, dancing, prose, poetry and other entertaining activities. Thus Bharata considers Krishna-Vishnu as the source of theatrical arts. Probably because of this Dhanajaya in his treatise *Dasharupaka* presents an interesting analogy between Vishnu-Krishna and Bharata. He says:

Dasharūpānukārēna yasya mādyanti bhāvakāh
Namah sarvavide tasmai Vishnave Bharatāyacha

The number of Vishnu's incarnations and kinds of play mentioned by Bharata is the same—i.e., ten. Both of them manifest in ten forms. This implies a close association of the *Bhāgavata* cult and theatrical arts.

Krishna is considered the presiding deity of *Chālikya Gandharva* by the *Harivansha Purāna* composed in 4th century A.D. The well known playwright Kālidāsa also refers to this mode of dramatic presentation in his play *Mālavikāgnimitram*. The *Harivansha Purāna* elaborately describes how a troupe of actresses enacted the life of Krishna in *Chālikya Gandharva* style. The occasion was a grand picnic arranged by the *Yādavas* at Pindārak Tirtha on the sea shore near Dwāraka. Through dance, drama and music the episodes from Krishna's life were enacted. This Purāna, belonging to the cult of *Bhāgavatas*, describes the dance-drama style in the following words:

Shubhāvaham Vruddhikaram Prashastam
Māngalyamēvātha tathā yashasyam
Punyam cha pushtyabhydayavaham
Nārāyanasyēshtamudārkīrtēh
Jayāvaham dharmabharāvaham cha
Duhswapnanasham parikīrtyamānam
Karōti pāpam cha yatha vihānti

Likewise the *Bhāgavata* cult has emphasised the religious significance of theatrical performances. By calling it auspicious and pious *Harivansha* further says that it fulfils desires, ensures victory, bestows success, removes ill effects of sins and confers religious merit. The *Bhāgavata* cult gave definite place to theatrical arts in their ritualistic practices.

The magico-religious significance of the *Rās* dance associated with the *Bhāgavata* cult is very well reflected in the Tamil epic *Shilappadhikāram* written around 2nd century A.D. In the 27th canto of the epic the dance of cowherdesses is described elaborately. It was performed to alleviate impending ill effects of the bad omens observed by an elderly cowherd lady Matari.

Her daughter informs her:

> Alas! The milk in the pot has not curdled. The beautiful eyes of the big humped bulls are full of tears; some calamity is happening. The fragrant butter in the pot does not melt. The lambs do not frisk about; some calamity is happening.
>
> Herds of cows with their four-nippled udders are shuddering and bellowing in fear; the big bells (tied to their necks) fall down. O! some calamity is happening.

The old lady says:

> Do not feel perturbed. To alleviate the grief of our cattle, we shall dance Kuravai (Rāskrida). Of the many boyhood games played by Mayavan (Krishna) and Balaram in Gokula, the kuravai was one. It was played by Mayavan with Pinnai (Radha) of long lance-like eyes.

Seven girls are selected for the ritual dance and they are arranged in a circle defining the position of each girl. One among them is called Krishna while yet another is Balaram. The snogs are sung, dances are performed. In the end it is said:

> May the deity celebrated in the Kuravai dance in which we were now engaged alleviate the distress which has befallen our cattles!

This significant statement throws light on the magico-religious nature of the *Rās* dance. Theatricals were offered to god to appease him. This reflects the attitude of *Bhāgavata* cult towards theatrical arts.

Rās is the most interesting dramatic dance which is associated with the cult of *Bhāgavatas*. Description of *Rās* dance is found in the collection of *Maharashtri Prakrit Gathas* by Hal Satavahana belonging to the early centuries of Christian era. A *gatha* from the collection, popularly known as *Gatha Saptashati*, says:

> While dancing with Krishna the smooth cheeks of cowherd girls became wet by the round drops of perspiration and in them started floating the reflections of sea-hued Krishna. A cowherd girl among the spectators came forward to whisper her appreciation in the ear of a dancer. When her lips brushed the cheek of the dancing girl the spectator cowherd girl enjoyed the bliss of kissing thousands of Krishna (floating in the drops of perspiration).

It is very interesting to note that it is for the first time Radha is mentioned by name as a beloved of Krishna in one of the *Gathas*.

Many Puranas including *Vishnu, Padma, Brahma* and *Brahmavaivarta* refer to the *Rās* dance. But it is the Bhāgavata Purana *Rās* which is most popular in the *Bhāgavata* cult. The whole episode can be divided into three parts. In the first part, Krishna plays on his flute and cowherd girls run to him in the deep woods of Vrindavana on the bank of river Yamuna. They dance with joy. In the second part Krishna disappears from among them as they are filled with pride. In his absence the cowherd girls enact many of his acts—*Leelas*—suffering the pangs of separation. In the third part Krishna takes pity on them and reappears on the scene. They again start dancing with joy. The whole episode includes dramatic enactment and dance. *Rās* is a circular dance performed by dark-hued Krishna with fair cowherd girls. Works on dramaturgy have also taken note of *Rās* as a dramatic dance, a kind of play.

Many interpretations are offered explaining the metaphysical significance of the *Rās* dance in the scheme of *Bhāgavata* philosophy. Let us confine to what *Bhāgavata Purāna* has said about it. The person who with deep faith listens to or describes the *Rās* episode is freed from carnal desire and lust and his heart becomes pure. He achieves *Para Bhakti* of the Lord. This is the result of *Rās* as a religious ritual.

A more significant fact is that the *Harivansha* and *Bhāgavata Purānas* contributed towards the evolution of Krishna drama and set the trend of enacting the episodes from Krishna's life. Through these religious books the cult of *Bhāgavata* encouraged theatrical activities for the propagation of their faith. *Bhāgavata Purāna* is more vocal about this. In the *Ekādasha Skandha* occurs the *Krishna-Uddhava* dialogue throwing light on the tenets of the *Bhāgavata* cult. Here, time and again, devotees are enjoined to arrange festivals full of dance, drama and music in honour of Krishna and Krishna speaks out:

Shradhālume kathā shrunvan subhadrā lōkapāvanī
Gāyannanusmaran karma janma chābhinayan
muhuh—11.11.23

(The faithful should sing and enact my story which is beautiful and auspicious. It sanctifies the people.)

Majjanmakarma kathānām mama parvānumōdanam
Gitatāndavavāditragōshtibhirmadgruhotsavah
—11.11.36

(The stories about my birth and life may be related. Joyous celebrations should be organised. Songs, dances, musical instruments should be offered to me on the festive occasions in my temples.)

Upagāyan grunan nrutyam karmānyabhinayan mama—11.27.44

(My story should be sung, danced and enacted on festive occasions.)

Annādyagītanrutyādi parvāni syurutanvaham
—11.27.35

(When festival is organised for me food, songs and dances should be offered to me.)

Pruthak satrena vā mahyam parvayātrā mahotsavan
Kārayēd gītanrutyādaimahārajvibhūtibhih—11.29.11

(Organise my festivals or Yatras in regal manner arranging performances of music and dance.)

This is the *Bhāgavata Dharma*, a joyous religion full of dance, music, songs and theatrical enactments. This positive attitude of the cult helped in the emergence of various theatrical forms all over the country based on the Krishna lore.

The *Bhāgavata Purāna* further enjoins the devotees to construct Krishna temples and donate land,

Theatre of Bhagavatas

income from markets, villages and cities to meet the expenditure of various rituals which naturally includes theatrical entertainments (11.27.50). In this context the stone inscription of king Sārangadeva dated Saka 1348 is worth mentioning. This inscription which was found at Anavada or Anahilapataka, a few miles from Patan, opens with a stanza from the *Dashāvatār Ashtapadi* of Jayadeva's well known Krishna opera – *Geeta Gōvinda*. At that time Maharajadhiraj Shri Sārangadeva of Vaghela dynasty was the ruler of Anahilapataka. It seems that there was a temple of Krishna at the place long before the reign of king Sārangadeva. The inscription makes a record of the gifts for worship, offerings and theatricals presented before Lord Krishna. The 7th line states that the donation was for—

(*Shri*) (*Kri*)*shnāpadānam*
(*Pu*) *ja Naivedya*
Prēkshanaka nimitta

Prēkshanaka means drama. It is clear from the inscription that Krishna plays were enacted at the temple of Anahilapataka and probably *Geeta Govinda* opera was also performed. We have already mentioned Bayana inscription of Chitralekha and passages from the *Bhāna Ubhayābhisarika* indicating the practice of staging plays at the Vishnu-Krishna temples.

Lord Jagannātha is identified with Krishna. His magnificent temple built by Anantvarma Chodagangadeva became the centre of *Bhāgavata* culture and art. The practice of staging plays at the *Yātrās* of Jagannātha is even older than his present temple at Puri. The tradition still continues. The *Geeta Govinda* opera composed by Jayadeva in the 12th century influenced Indian theatrical tradition in a big way. It describes the amorous lives of Radha and Krishna. Inscription of Gajapati ruler Pratāprudradeva dated July 1499 says:

> Dancing will be performed at the Bhoga (food offering) time of the elder Thakur (Balarāma) and Geeta Govinda Thakur (Jagannātha—Krishna). This dancing will be held from the end of evening Dhupa up to the time of Bada Singar (bed-time) Dhupa. The batch (dancing girls) of Bada Thakura, the fixed female dancers of Kapilēshvar Thakura, the old batch, the Telengi batch, all will learn no other song than *Geeta Govinda* of Bada Thakura. They will not sing any other song. No other kind of dancing should be performed before the god. Besides dancing there are four Vaishnava singers, they will sing only the Geeta Govinda. Hearing in one tone from them, those who are ignorant will learn the Geeta Govinda song, they should not learn any other song. The superintendent who knowingly allows other song to be sung, and other dancing to be performed rebels against Jagannatha.

Many similar inscriptions and literary references can be cited to indicate the long and continuous tradition of *Bhāgavata* theatre in all parts of the country. In the famous Krishna temple of Guruvāyur *Krishnan Attam* cycle of plays are regularly enacted. *Geeta Govinda* is still sung and performed in the Puri temple of Jagannātha.

It is very significant to note the magico-religious or ritualistic aspect which these dramatic performances have retained. The play *Swayamvaram* in the

Krishnan Attam series is offered to Guruvayurappa (Krishna) to obtain a good husband; likewise *Avatāram* is offered to beget a child. In the *Rās* plays of Vraj after the make-up the child actors acting as Krishna, Radha etc. are treated as deities themselves. People prostrate before them, seek their blessings. From the make-up room to the stage and back they are carried on shoulders. They are worshipped as idols of deities in the temples. The same rituals are observed on the stage.

The *Bhāgavata* cult gave a great impetus to Indian theatre in general.

Rupa Goswami, author of three Krishna plays— *Vidagdha Mādhav*, *Lalit Mādhav* and *Danakēli Kaumudi*—was a disciple of Chaitanya Mahāprabhu. He settled in the Vraj region and wrote a work on dramaturgy called *Nātakachandrika*, in the 16th century. It is very much based on *Bhāgavata* theatre. He states therein that of all kinds of dramatic heroes, Krishna is the best. In his work *Bhaktirasāmritasindhu* Rupa says that poetry and drama based on Krishna help the growth of a newly emerged feeling of Krishna-devotion in the mind of a person.

Nave ratānkure jāte Haribhaktasya kasyachit
Vibhāvatvādihetutwam kincitkāyyanatyavoh

He further says that the sins of several births can be eliminated by dancing joyfully before Krishna.

As we have seen earlier Krishna is associated with many classical and folk dances, theatre forms like *Rās*, *Hallisaka*, *Chalikya Gandharva*. Bharata in his

Nātyashāstra narrates a story of his fight with demons *Madhu* and *Kaitabha*. Hari killed them with varied, pure, expressive and graceful *Angaharas—Vichitraivirshadaih sphutaih salalitairapi Angahāraih* - and also forceful *Chāris—Samrambhavegabahulaināchari*. *Angahāra* is a major dance movement composed of smaller units known as *Karanas*. The combined movement of hands and feet striking a particular dance-posture is called *Karana*. According to *Nātyashāstra* there are 32 *Angahāras* and 108 *Karanas*. Bharata has devoted one full chapter to explain *Chāris* which are 32 in number. He defines *Chāri* as moving simultaneously feet, shanks and the hip— *Evam pādasya janghāyā ūroh katyāsthathaiva cha samānākaranā cchestha*. This explains Krishna's association with classical dance. *Bhāgavata Purāna* describes his *Tāndava*, a forceful dance, performed on the hood of the ferocious cobra *Kāliya*. On the occasion celestial musicians came down to the earth with their orchestra and played on various musical instruments. Classical Kathak dance style emanated from this dance of Krishna. His influence on other classical dance styles of India including *Manipuri*, *Rās*, *Odissi* and *Bharatnātyam* is quite evident.

It is very interesting to note that at the Shārangapani temple of Kumbhakonam Krishna is shown in many dance stances—*Karanas*. Dr. C. Sivaramamurthi in the fifth chapter of his book *Nataraja* has discussed the *Vaishnavite version of Shaivite* (*Karana*) *series* which we see sculpted on many temples including Brihadeshvar temple at Tanjore and Shiva temple at Chidambaram. He has identified all the *Karanas* which include *Dikvāsika Karana*, *Nikunchita Karana*, *Dandapaksha Karana*, *Lalātatilaka Karana*, *Dandarēchita Karana* etc. The *Krishna Karana* series in the Chola temple of 12th-13th century A.D. is very fascinating and recognises the role and contribution of Krishna to *Natya*—theatre.

Association of theatrical arts with the cult of Krishna has been acknowledged by many scholars. Some tried to trace the origin of Indian theatre to Krishna cult while some agreed that it made a significant contribution to the evolution of theatre in India. We have already quoted E.P. Horrowitz on the subject. Sylvain Levi opines:

> The first document which positively attests the existence of dramatic representations in India associates the new art with the legend of Krishna. The association may have been a mere accident, yet it would not be difficult to give a rational justification for it. No other divinity deserves more to preside over the birth of the Indian drama than the young and brilliant hero, lover of Gopis and vanquisher of demons. The cult of Krishna has been intimately associated with the history of the drama during long centuries. In the Middle Ages, it gave to the moribund theatre a new lease of life, and, in the present day, it gave birth to a new type of drama.

Sten Konow agrees with Lassen that 'the land of Sūrasena is the home of the Indian drama'. Horrowitz states: 'The Agra district is the holy land of Krishnaism.' Professor Ridgeway tries to find the origin of Indian theatre in the performances held in honour of the dead, including Krishna. This shows the role played by the *Bhāgavata* cult based on Krishna worship in the evolution of Indian theatre.

DASHĀVATĀR

THE *Bhāgvad Purāna* states: 'Just as from an inexhaustible lake thousands of streams flow on all sides so also from Hari come forth countless incarnations.' Creation, preservation and destruction constitute an eternal cycle of existence. Hari, that is Vishnu, represents the principle of preservation and continuity of life. He is a supreme being, sublime source of eternal bliss, the entire universe is just a manifestation of his power. 'God creates this world, enters into it and like an actor who assumes different roles on the stage performs various acts.' (*Bhāgvad Purāna*). He assumes many forms to destroy evil, protect the good and restore the glory of *Dharma* (*Gita* 4.8). There are many references to his incarnations in ancient literature. Though their number differs from book to book (*Matsya Purana* 10; *Ahirbudhnya Samhita* 39; *Bhāgavat Purāna* 24; *Nārāyanīya* section of *Mahābhārata* 6 etc.) they are generally considered to be ten. The main incarnations of Vishnu are *Matsya* (Fish), *Kūrma* (Tortoise), *Varāha* (Boar), *Nrusimha* (Lion-man), *Vāman*, *Parashurām*, *Rām*, *Krishna* (or *Balarāma*), *Buddha* and *Kalki*. These ten incarnations are called *Dashāvatār*.

The myths associated with some of these incarnations are found in Vedic literature. The root of *Vāmanāvatār* story can be traced back to *Rigveda* and

Shatapatha Brāhmana. According to later *Brāhmanas* and *Āranyakas* it was Prajāpati who assumed the forms of fish, tortoise and boar. The *Taittiriya Āranyaka* says that the earth was raised out of primordial waters by Prajāpati in the form of a hundred armed black boar. As per *Shatapatha Brāhmana* it was Prajāpati in the form of a fish who saved Manu from the great deluge. As Vishnu, who was a rather insignificant deity in Vedic times, grew in stature these mythical accounts were transferred to his name by his devotees. Epics and *Puranas* gave shape to the *avatāra* concept and formed a cluster of mythology around each incarnation. The cult of *Bhāgavatas* started spreading all over the land. Heliodorus, the Greek ambassador to the court of Sunga king Kautsiputra Bhagabhadra erected a thirty-foot high monolithic Garuda pillar in honour of Vasudeva in the 2nd century B.C. and proclaimed himself *'Bhāgavata'*. The patronage of Gupta emperors gave an impetus to the *Bhāgavata* cult. Chandra Gupta II was a devout Vaishnava and he assumed the title *'Pāmara-Bhāgavata'* to announce his religious leanings. The Vishnu temple at Deogarh buit around 500 A.D. is known as Dashāvatār temple. Māmallapuram inscription of eighth century A.D. mentions ten incarnations of Vishnu. The well-known Kailāsha temple and Dashāvatār cave at Ellora bear the sculptural representation of some of the *avatāras* of Vishnu. There are numerous inscriptions and epigraphs referring to the one or many incarnations. We find many panels depicting divine incarnations. One such panel is in the Bharatpur Museum. The worship of Dashāvatār took many forms in the course of time. Malla kings of Vishnupur are credited with the invention of Dashāvatār playing cards, round in shape. The pack of 120 cards is divided into 10 groups each bearing the name of one of the incarnations of Vishnu. *Bhavishya* and *Vishnu Purānas* tell us about *Dashāvatār Vrata* when the images of ten incarnations are worshipped for attaining Vishnulok after death.

Though the Krishna-drama is quite ancient, it is rather difficult to state exactly when the *Dashāvatār* drama as such came into being. However *Purānas* do prescribe the use of dance, drama and music to appease the gods. In fact, according to tradition, drama is the best service one can offer to Vishnu. Bharata also agrees with this. He says:

> The gods are never so pleased on being worshipped with scents and garlands, as they are delighted with the performance of dramas (XXXVI. 81-2).

In the *Bhāgavata Purāna* Vishnu says that the devotees should on festive religious occasions enact his *leelas* before his image in the temple. A 10th century inscription refers to *Prēksha* presented before the idol of Vishnu by the talented dancing girls of exceptional beauty and grace. It says:

> Owing to the temptation of seeing the beautiful dancing girls the enemy of Madhu (Vishnu) does not leave his own image for a moment (Ep. Ind., Vol. XXII, p. 124).

Another inscription refers to a grant made by the king to a temple for performing plays—*Prēkshanakas*—

Dashāvatār

before Lord Shrikrishna (I.A., Vol. XLI, 1912, p. 20). *Ubhayābhisārika Bhān* of Vararuchi refers to a musical play performed in the temple of Bhagavān Nārāyan Vishnu. *Rājatarangini* mentions the tradition of performing dances in the temple of Keshava (4. 269-274). An inscription attached to Anant Vasudeo temple at Bhuvaneshvar speaks about a hundred deer-eyed girls adept in the arts of dancing and singing. Naturally the stories associated with ten incarnations of Vishnu must have been transformed into musical dance-dramas for presentation. However it is around the 12th century that we find positive literary evidence indicating the existence of a dance-performance based on the *Dashāvatār* theme as such. We also have inscriptional evidence to show that such dance used to be performed in the Nata Mandir of a well-known temple.

In the 12th century the great poet Jayadeva composed his immortal dramatic poem *Gita Govinda*. The Ganga rulers of the time were staunch Vaishnavites. The Puri temple of Lord Jagannātha became a great centre of Vaishnava art and culture during their rule. According to tradition Jayadeva's wife Padmāvati was a temple dancer who used to perform the poem before the lord. *Prithvirāj Rāso* calls Jayadeva the '*Kavirāyam*', king among poets, and further says that he always used to sing in praise of Govinda and Govinda alone.

In the first *Sarga* of Jayadeva's *Gita Govinda* we find an *ashtapadi* dedicated to the ten incarnations of Lord.Vishnu.. Jayadeva has described in ten stanzas the incarnations of Vishnu with a great sense of devotion. He mentions Balarāma as one of the incarnations of Keshava. It is a well-known fact that Jayadeva composed this poem to be danced out before Lord Jagannātha at Puri. The *Dashāvatār Ashtapadi* appears at the beginning of the poem and forms the *Purvaranga* of the dance-drama. The tradition of presenting *Dashāvatār* dance as a part of *Gita Govinda* dance-drama continued for centuries at Puri. The Gajapati ruler Pratāprudradeva's inscription at Jagannātha temple (July 1499 A.D.) specifically states that *Gita Govinda* and *Gita Govinda Nat* only should be performed before the deity by the dancing girls. With the spread of *Gita Govinda* the *Dashāvatār Ashtapadi* also became quite popular. It may be noted here that in the *Purvaranga* of *Kathakali* of Kerala a song from *Gita Govinda* is invariably sung. Selections from the poem are sung. Scholars have found a manuscript of *Gita Govinda* with full instructions to the dancers in the Saraswati Mahal Library at Tanjore (*Gita Govinda with Abhinaya:* Ed. K. Vasudeva Sastri). There are evidences to indicate that in many parts of India the dance-drama of Jayadeva became quite popular and influenced local dramatic forms. According to some scholars *Krishnanattam* of Kerala is one such example. *Dashāvatār Ashtapadi* also became quite popular and probably its popularity might have inspired some creative minds to start the tradition o *Dashāvatāri* plays.

In the *Abhinayadarpana* of Acharya Nandikeshvara Dashāvatār *hasta mudras* are given. By these hand-gestures a dancer can indicate various incarnations of Vishnu. There is some uncertainty about the date

Dashāvatār

of *Abhinayadarpana*. Scholars have assigned different dates varying from 5th to 12th century A.D. to this treatise. Nandikeshvara does not mention Buddhāvatār. If one accepts the premise that the treatise is written well before the time when Buddha was included in the *avatāra* pantheon we can place it in the 5th century. The first mention of Buddha in the *avatāra* cycle is found in the 6th century *Matsya Purāna*. But at the same time one cannot rule out the possibility of Acharya Nandikeshvara being averse to the idea of the inclusion of Buddha in the *avatāra* pantheon. Taking these and other relevant factors into consideration some scholars have suggested the 12th century as the possible date of the treatise. This means Acharya wrote his treatise in the same century in which Jayadeva composed his dramatic poetry. Was Nandikeshvara aware of Jayadeva's *Ashtapadi* on *Dashāvatār*? However it may be noted that Jayadeva has accepted Buddha as one of the divine incarnations. It may also be noted that both of them have accepted Balarama as an *avatāra* of Vishnu. *Dashāvatār hasta mudras* given by Acharya Nandikeshvara are as follows:

Matsya Hasta Mudra : One palm on another, both pointing downwards, both the thumbs and little fingers spread out, hands at shoulder height (216, 196).

Kūrma : All fingers extended straight and joined together is *Patak Hasta Mudra*. When the

	thumb of *Patak Hasta* is separated and extended out it is *Ardhachandra Hasta*. Both palms in *Ardhachandra* joined together freeing little finger and thumb is *Kurma Hasta* (93, 197, 217). Hands at shoulder height.
Varāha	: The middle of the *Patak* hand is hollowed, thumb and little finger extended is *Mrigashīrsha*, both the palms in *Mrigashīrsha*, little finger of one *MS* touching thumb of another *MS* (139, 198, 218).
Nrusimha	: The tips of the middle and the third fingers are applied to the thumbs and the rest extended is *Simha Mukha* (142). Right hand in *SM Mudra* and left in *Tripatak Mudra*. When third finger of *Patak* is bent it is *Tripatak* (142, 100, 219).
Vāmana	: The four fingers are bent into the palm and the thumb is set on them is *Mushti* (fist), when one fist is held above another it is *Vāmana* (116, 220).
Parashurāma	: Left hand on hips and right in *Ardha Patak*. A little

Dashāvatār

	finger of *Tripatak* also bent is *Ardhapatak* (103, 221).
Rāma	: Left hand in *Kapittha Mudra* and right in *Shikhara Mudra*. If the thumb of *Mushti* is raised it is *Shikhara*. The forefinger of the *Shikhara* hand bent over the top of the thumb is *Kapittha* elephant apple (118, 121, 222).
Balarāma	: Right hand in *Patak* and left in *Mushti Hasta Mudra* (223).
Krishna	: Both the hands in *Mrigashirsha* facing each other; held in front of the mouth (224).
Kalki	: Right hand in *Patak* and left in *Tripatak Mudra* (225).

This is the *Dashāvatār* iconography of dance as devised by Acharya Nandikeshvara around the 12th century. It is possible that the *Dashāvatār* dance might have formed part of the *Purvaranga* proceedings of the Vaishnava dramas performed in the temples. *Purvaranga* of *Gita Govinda* is an excellent example. It may be noted here that in one of the *Ankia* plays of Mahāpurusha Shankardeva of Assam (1449-1568 A.D.) the *Mukti Mangal Bhatima*, that is, benedictory verse, is devoted to the *Dashāvatār*. This clearly indicates the influence of Jayadeva. This Bhatima from Keli Gopal Nat is presented in a *Satriya* dance style as a separate item and is known as *Dashāvatāri* dance.

The Marathi saint-poet Ramdas who was a contemporary of Shivaji refers to *Dashāvatāri* plays in his well known work *Dasbodha*. He states:

Khelata netake Dashavatari
Tethe yeti sundar nari
Netra modati kalakusari
Pari avaghe dhatingana — Dasbodha 6-8-11

In the *Dashāvatāri* play beautiful girls come on the stage and enchant the audience with the movements of their eyes. But in reality they are all male actors. From this verse we come to know that at the time of Ramdas there was a tradition of staging *Dashāvatāri* plays and female roles were done by male actors. Around this time *Yakshagāna* theatre emerged in Karnataka. These *Yakshagāna* plays are also known as *Dashāvatār Ata*. *Yakshagāna* plays are called *Dashāvatār Ata* because they present the mythical stories connected with the ten incarnations of Lord Vishnu. The earliest available *Yakshagāna* play *Virātparva* is datable to 1564 A.D. Though known as *Dashāvatār Ata* they do not depict the cycle of ten incarnations in a single play. However in the *Mangal geet* sung at the end of the *Yakshagāna* plays the *Dashāvatārs* are mentioned and propitiated. This is positive evidence connecting *Yakshagāna* with the tradition of Dashāvatār plays.

As we have seen earlier the manuscript of *Gita Govinda* was found in the Saraswati Mahal Library at Tanjore in the distant south. Maratha rulers of Tanjore were not only great patrons of art and culture but they themselves were writers of outstanding merit. The second Maratha ruler of Tanjore, Shahraj Bhosale (1684-1711 A.D.) wrote many plays in Telugu, Hindi, Tamil and Marathi. He was rightly known as *Kavibhoja*. One of his plays *Panchabhāshavilas* is written in five languages. Five heroines of the play representing different languages sing a song in praise of the ten incarnations of Vishnu. This song is clearly inspired by the *Dashāvatār Ashtapadi* of Jayadeva. In his play *Hariharavilās* the *Sutradhār* calls himself *Bhāgavat Dashāvatāri*. 'You fool, you are alone. What do you mean by *Dashāvatār*?', asks the surprised *Kanchuki*. Replying to his query *Sutradhār* states: 'Friend, I alone take all the roles of the ten avatārs', a reference to the tradition of presenting the *Dashāvatār* dance by an actor in the *Purvaranga* of the Vaishnava plays or he might have actually presented himself on stage in ten different costumes representing the ten incarnations.

This indicates for certain that in the dance-dramas of Bhāgavatas many a time the *Dashāvatār* item was included. At first the tradition might have started with the presentation of the *Dashāvatār* song by the actor utilising gesture-language to underline its meaning in visual terms. Later on the mythical story connected with any one or two incarnations might have been enacted in addition to the *Dashāvatār* song which subsequently became a part of *Purvaranga*.

In certain parts of the country the tradition of *Dashāvatār* plays developed on different lines. Here all the ten Avatārs are brought on the stage one after another and episodes connected with the major incarnations were presented elaborately. The remains of this tradition still linger in the Konkan area of Maharashtra and the adjoining region of Goa. These plays are known as *Dashāvatār* plays and as their name indicates these plays present all the ten incarnations of Vishnu on stage.

The coastal region of Goa and Konkan is known from ancient times as a cradle of dramatic arts. The Tamil classic *Shilappadhikāram* mentions Konkan actors and dancers who entertained the Chera King Sanguttuvan. Vaishnava drama flourished in the region under the patronage of temple institutions. *Jagar* is the oldest extant dramatic form of Goa. Rich in metaphysical content it presents the mythical story of slaying demons Madhu and Kaitabha by Vishnu. According to *Natyashastra* the Lord killed the demons with varied pure, expressive, and graceful *angahāras*. The *vrittis* emerged out of this combat (*NS*, 22, 1-16). *Ranamale, Tratika, Putana, Virabhadra, Balakrida Kala, Gaulan Kala, Gopal Kala* are some of the dramatic forms of Goa connected with the *Dashāvatār* themes.

The prevalent dance forms like *Goff* and *Rās* are also connected with the *Krishnāvatār* of Vishnu. These plays are presented at temple festivals and *Jātrās*. *Dashāvatār* is the most developed dramatic form of the region. According to some scholars it came to Goa from Karnataka. Goa and Karnataka were under the Vijayanagar empire from A.D. 1367 to 1468. Up to 1781 some parts of Goa were under Kanaree Sondkar rulers. Though the *Yakshagana* of Karnataka is known as *Dashāvatār Ata* there is hardly any resemblance between *Dashāvatār Ata* of Karnataka and *Dashāvatār* of Goa and Konkan except that we find some Kannada words and songs included in *Dashāvatār* plays. All the forms of Vaishnava drama are interrelated in the sense that they are regional variations of the countrywide theatre movement inspired by the *Bhāgavata* cult. *Krishnan Attam* and *Kathakali* of Kerala, *Yakshagāna* of Karnataka, *Kuchipudi* of Andhra, *Bhāgavatamēla* of Tamil Nadu, *Ankia Nat* of Assam, *Leela* plays of Uttar Pradesh, *Rās* of Gujarat and Manipur belong to the same tradition. These are in one way or another connected with *Dashāvatār* themes, though their execution differs. In the *Rās leela* of Vrindavan sometimes the ten incarnations are shown on the stage. In the *Kuchipudi* play *Bhāmā Kalāpam* the heroine Satyabhama while describing Krishna mentions his ten incarnations and shows all of them on the stage through dance and *abhinaya*. This portion is known as *Dashāvatārābhinayam*. *Lalit* is the most ancient dramatic form of Maharashtra in which *Dashāvatārs* are mentioned in the *Purvaranga*. Of all the dramatic forms mentioned above the *Dashāvatār* of Goa and Konkan is unique in the sense that in it efforts are made to accommodate in a single performance as many of the incarnations as possible. Of course some of the incarnations like *Matsyāvatār*, *Nrusimhāvatār*, *Vāmanāvatār*, *Rāmāvatār* and *Krishnāvatār* are played prominently. The play, after elaborate *Purvaranga*, opens with the *Matsyāvatār*. Demon Sankāsura steals the *Vedas* from Brahma, and Vishnu after killing the demon recovers them.

Sankāsura of *Dashāvatār* is the villain and the jester combined in one. Buddha and Kalki incarnations are not shown on the stage. Actors in the guise of Parashurām, Kurma and Varāha do appear on the stage but no episode related to these incarnations is shown on the stage. Dramatised episodes from Rāma and Krishna incarnations occupy an important position in the scheme of the *Dashāvatār* play. The tradition of presenting *Dashāvatāri* plays in temples still lingers in Goa, though in quite an abridged form. Sometimes the show ends with *Matsyāvatār*. This portion of the play is called *Sankāsura Kala* also.

Krishna-drama is at least as old as the *Bālacharitam* of Bhasa. This play written about 400 B.C. in its opening *shloka* mentions some of the incarnations of Vishnu like Nārāyana, Vishnu-Vāman, Rām and Krishna. In the play *Karnābharan* he has mentioned the *Nrusimhāvatār*—man-lion incarnation. The concept of incarnations of Vishnu, as we have seen earlier, grew with time. Dr. Haraprasad Shastri in his 'Note on Vishnupur Circular Cards' (Journal of the Asiatic Society of Bengal, Vol. LXIV, No. 3, 1895, p. 284-85) opines that 'the antiquity of orthodox list (of *Dashāvatārs*) goes back to Jayadeva in the 12th and Kshemendra in 11th century.' We may give the credit of bringing *Dashāvatār* concept into the fold of theatrical arts to Jayadeva and certainly the credit of developing it into a full-fledged dramatic form goes to the people of Goa and Konkan.

DANCE-WORSHIP OF STUPAS

IN its primordial form the stupa, *thupa* in Prakrit, was a simple funebrial mound of earth with a wooden stick inserted on its summit. It was raised over the mortal remains of a revered person and worshipped in his sacred memory. Generally domical in shape these monuments underwent many conceptual and architectural changes since their inception. It came to be associated mainly with Buddhist creed and the credit of making the cult of stupa popular is given to Emperor Ashoka. However in the *Maha Parinibbana Sutta* Buddha himself has vouched for its antiquity in a conversation with his close associate and disciple Ananda. In brief, the dialogue between the two runs as follows:

Ananda : What we are to do, Lord, with the remains of the Tathagata?

Buddha : Hinder not yourself, Ananda, by honouring the remains of Tathagata.

Ananda : What should be done, Lord, with the remains of the Tathagata?

Buddha : As men treat the remains of a king of kings, so, Ananda, should they treat the remains of a Tathagata.

Ananda : And how, Lord, do they treat the remains of the king of kings (Chakravarti Raja)?

Buddha : They built a funeral pile of all kinds of perfumes, and burn the body of the king of kings. And then at four crossroads they erect a *Thupa*

> to the king of kings. This, Ananda, is the
> way in which they treat the remains of a king
> of kings ... And whosoever shall there place
> garlands or perfumes or paint or make saluta-
> tion there, or become in its presence calm in
> heart—that shall long be to them for a profit
> and a joy.

He further states that the hearts of many would be made calm and happy in the presence of stupa and hence they would be reborn after death in the happy realms of heaven.

It is clear from the dialogue that Buddha was aware of the custom of raising a memorial stupa which was in vogue well before him. In fact we see the early glimpses of this custom in the 18th *Sukta* of the 10th *Mandala* of *Rigveda*. The hymn says:

> Go to thy mother, this earth, the widely extending, very
> gracious Prithvi. That maiden, soft as wool to the pious,
> may protect thee from the abode of destruction.

This refers to burial of the dead body. It also states about raising an earthen mound over the spot and inserting in its top a wooden stick—*sthuna*—for the god of death Yama to inhabit.

It is evident from many references in the early Vedic literature that even the charred remains of the dead body after consigning it to flames were buried by putting them in urns. In this context it is interesting to refer to *Yajurveda* (35/15), *Vajasaneyi Samhita* (18/1/3), *Shatapatha Brahmana* (13/8/3/11) and *Ramayana* (5/22/29). In the *Mahabharata's Sabha*

Dance-Worship of Stupas

Parva Krishna sitting on his bird-vehicle Garuda is compared with the stick—*Chaitya Yupa*—raised on the top of *Chaitya*. Stupas are also referred as *Chaityas* in literature and inscriptions. *Sujata Jataka* and *Mahakapi Jataka* also refer to the cult of stupa, raising memorial mound over the mortal remains of a dead person. In fact this is a universal practice.

Hollow rock-cut cave tombs of Vedic period were found in South India. According to G. Jouveau-Dubreuil the best specimen of it is available at Mannapuram in Kerala. Describing the cave in his work *Vedic Antiquities* he says:

> The principal part (of the cave) is formed of a vault perfectly hemispherical and neatly cut in rocks. In the centre is the column cut in the same rock.

Scholars refer to the cave as hollowed stupa. It is called as 'perfect specimen of a Vedic stupa of the pre-Buddhist era'.

Lauriya Nandangarh is a place famous for Ashokan pillar of great beauty. Here somewhat hemispherical burial mounds were found. Dated to pre-Mauryan era these mounds are considered as royal tombs. In the Archaeological Report 1966-7 T. Bloch writes:

> I found here at depth of six to twelve feet a small deposit of human bones mixed up with charcoal and a small gold leaf with a figure of a standing figure.

This figure was identified as that of Prithvi, deity

earth. He further informs us that the mound consists of layers of earth or clay, raised around a wooden post, just as the funeral monuments referred to in Vedic verse:

> I raise the earth around thee; that I lay down this lump of earth ... may the manes hold this pillar for thee and may Yama prepare a seat for thee in the other world.

Lauriya mounds may be described as specimens of early funernal mounds which later developed into magnificent stupas associated with the creed of Buddha.

According to *Maha Parinibbana Sutta* after the death of Buddha stupas were raised on the portions of his charred remains. It is said that Emperor Ashoka (*c.* 273-236 B.C.) opened these stupas and distributed the mortal remains of Buddha all over the country to construct many more stupas on them. Their number is said to be eightyfour thousand. Chinese pilgrims like Fa-hien and Hiuen Tsang have described some of them in their accounts. I-tsing writes:

> The priests and the laymen in India make *chaityas* with earth, or impress the Bdddha's image on silk or paper and worship it with offerings whenever they go. Sometimes they built stupas of Buddha by making a pile and surrounding it with bricks.
> —*A Record of Buddhist Religion*, p. 150

One of the stupas constructed by Ashoka is at Sanchi. It is in the best state of preservation. However the simple original mound of bricks underwent many changes in subsequent centuries and it is now a most ornate and beautiful structure. Tracing its structural evolution Dr. Debala Mitra writes:

> The stupa of Ashoka underwent enlargement with an encasing of dressed stones in the Shunga period which also saw the construction of drum-balustrade and the ground-balustrade, the latter around the processional path at the ground level. In the first century B.C. were added four gateways, which, with their rich texture vibrant with lavish carvings, are unique of their kind.

Stupas of Bharhut, Amaravati, Jaggayyapeta are some of the famous Buddhist structures though not in equally good state of preservation. The carvings on these ancient monuments give us an idea of contemporary social and religious life. They also give us a clue to the fact that music and dancing formed part of stupa worship.

It is very interesting to note that in the 18th *Sukta* of the 10th *Mandala* of *Rigveda* where we first find the description of funebrial mound, that ultimately evolved into magnificent stupas, we also find that dancing and singing was a part of funeral rituals. Its third *Shloka* says:

> Divided from the dead are these, the living: now be our calling on God be successful. We have gone forth for dancing (*Nataye*) and for laughter (*Hasaya*), to further times prolonging our existence.

This Rigvedic tradition of including dance in funeral rites it seems was preserved by the Mallas of

Kusinara where Buddha breathed his last. *Maha Parinibbana Sutta* informs us:

> Then (after the death of Buddha) the Mallas of Kusinara gave orders to their attendants, saying, 'Gather together perfumes and garlands, and all the music in Kusinara.'
>
> And the Mallas of Kusinara took the perfumes and garlands, and all the musical instruments, and five hundred suits of apparel, and went to Upavattana, to the Sala grove of the Mallas, where the body of the Blessed One lay. There they passed the day in paying honour, reverence, respect, and homage to the remains of the Blessed One with dancing and hymns, and music, and with garlands and perfumes; and in making canopies of their garments, and preparing decoration wreaths to hang thereon.
>
> Then the Mallas of Kusinara thought: 'It is much too late to burn the body of the Blessed One today. Let us now perform the cremation tomorrow.' And in paying honour, reverence, respect and homage to the remains of the Blessed One with dancing, and hymns, and music and with garlands and perfumes; and in making canopies of their garments, and preparing decoration wreaths to hang thereon, they passed the second day too, and then the third day and the fourth, and the fifth and the sixth day also.
>
> Then on the seventh day the Mallas of Kusinara thought: 'Let us carry the body of the Blessed One, by the south and outside, to a spot on the south, and outside of the city, paying it honour, and reverence, and respect, and homage, with dance, song and music, with garlands and perfumes, and there to the south of the city, let us perform the cremation ceremony.'
>
> Then (after burning the body of Buddha) the Mallas of Kusinara surrounded the bones of the Blessed One in their Council Hall with a lattice work of spears and with a rampart of bows; and then for seven days they paid honour and reverence and respect and homage to them

Dance-Worship of Stupas

with dance and song and music, and with garlands and perfumes.

Obviously they must have been singing the songs depicting the life of Buddha translating them into dances, culminating the whole thing into a kind of theatrical spectacle and festivity. The Buddhist work *Avadanshataka* mentions a performance of *Buddha Nataka*, a play based on the life of Buddha, staged at the command of the king of Shobhavati by a *Natacharya* (dance-master) of Dakshinapatha. This points at the tradition of staging plays, operas based on the themes taken from the life of Buddha. The Mallas of Kusinara might have presented similar performances through dance, song and music to celebrate the *Mahanirvan* of their Lord.

It seems that early stupa-worship included dancing and singing and music. The best illustration of this is found sculptured on the west pillar of the northern gateway of Sanchi stupa. Sir John Marshall describes the panel as follows:

> The feast was celebrated by the Mallas of Kusinagara in honour of their share of the Buddha's relics. The stupa in which they were deposited has no less than two terraces and three railings, the outermost of which is adorned with a *Torana* (Gateway) with double lintel. In the air as many as four kinnaras are paying it worship with garlands; as far as the human worshippers, they are going round it in procession at a sort of dance step, few inside but greater number outside the first balustrade. Some are clapping their hands, one is waving a standard, others are bringing offerings of flowers, while in foreground

thunders an orchestra consisting of a harp, a kettledrum, two sorts of tambourine (cylindrical and ovoid), a double flute and two curved trumpets whose mouths are shaped like serpent heads.

Sculptural and literary evidences collaborate to indicate the tradition of inclusion of dance, song and music in the ritual worship of Buddhist monuments. On the left pillar of the West Gateway there is a beautiful sculpture showing Nagas worshipping the throne of Buddha under a Pipal tree. Here we see beautiful Naga girls dancing on the accompaniment of an orchestra consisting of musical instruments like flute, harp and elongated drums. We find yet another significant sculptural representation of offering dance worship on the South Gateway pillar. Here in centre is Buddha's head-dress kept on the throne in a tray. One person is holding royal umbrella over it with great respect. Some people, forming a chorus, are sitting near the place of worship singing hymns. Among them is standing a very lovely dancer in an enchanting posture. She is showing a very curvacious and graceful *hasta-mudra*. Her supple body, thin waist adds to her charm. She is offering dance-worship to the relic of Buddha.

According to Buddhist scriptures after his great departure, or *Mahabhinishkramana*, from home he cut off his hair and threw them up along with his turban. They were borne by the deities to the heaven called *Trayastrimsa*. On a railing post of the Bharhut stupa, now in Calcutta Museum, a scene is sculptured showing the three storeyed building with the words *Vejayato prasade* (or Vaijayanta palace) inscribed on it. Adjoining to it is a building with domical roof with the inscription *Sudhamma devasabha* and *Bhagavato chudamaho*. Chudamaho means the festival in honour of the hair-lock of Lord Buddha, which is enshrined in the *Devasabha*. It is in a way a kind of stupa or temple with the relic of Buddha. In front of it we see four dancers dancing joyously accompanied by an orchestra. This scene also shows that festivity at Buddhist monuments included dancing, singing and music, obviously related to the Buddhist themes.

We will cite here one more significant evidence of dance-worship sculptured on the Prasenjit pillar of the Bharhut stupa. Here we see four heavenly damsels dancing before a Bodhi tree. An eight-member musical orchestra is seen in attendance. The scene bears the following inscription:

Sadika sammadam turam devanam
Alambusa acchara
Misakesi acchara
Padumavati acchara
Subhada acchara

It means: 'A jovial ravishing music of the gods, gay with dramatic acting by dancing nymphs Alambusa, Misakesi, Padumavati and Subhada.' The musical opera is being performed before a Bodhi tree which is a symbol of Buddha. This scene also clearly establishes the strong tradition of including dancing, music and singing in the ritual worship of Buddhist monuments including stupa, Bodhi tree etc. Many more similar examples can be cited from different sculptured panels of different stupas. The association of Yakshas with Buddhist stupas itself is a valid evidence of people offering theatricals before them as a part of worship. Yakshas are appeased with music and theatricals.

Sylvain refers to the Ceylonese tradition of presenting musical operas before stupas as a part of festivity and Buddha worship. He informs us that early Buddhist kings like Dutthagamani inaugurated the Mahathupo by arranging dancing and singing. His brother named Mahadatthiko is also shown celebrating the laying down of foundation of stupa by presenting theatricals. He made dances and tableaus to be presented and music to be sung and played. Finally he orders 'the gods playing instruments' to appear on the dagoba or stupa (*The Theatre of India*, Vol. II, p. 34).

The tradition of theatrical worship of Buddha and organising musical festivals in his honour lingered for centuries in China and Tibet. Still in the Buddhist monasteries of the Himalayan region of India plays are enacted before the Lord.

APPENDIX A

REFERENCES TO TEMPLE THEATRE IN INSCRIPTIONS

(1) *A.R.Ep., 1916, No. B 557: Paṭṭamaḍai, Tirunelveli district, Tamil Nadu. Tamil. Pāṇḍya Jaṭāvarman *alias* Tribhuvanachakravartin Vīrapāṇḍyadēva, year 3.

'Registers that the Śrī Rudras, Śrī Mahēśvaras and the Dēvakannis of the temple of Śīvallīśuvaramuḍaiyār at Paṭṭamaḍai granted 1 *mā* of land and certain privileges in the temple to the temple dancing girl Uyyavandāḷ Aḷagiyaśōdi *alias* Vīrasēkhara-nangai, for enacting the drama on some festival days.'

(2) *A.R.Ep.*, 1921, No. 42, also pt. 2, para 68: Big Conjeevaram, Chingleput district, Tamil Nadu. Tamil. Śambuvarāya, year 17.

'This number contains some interesting information in respect of certain licences granted to a troupe of actors who claimed the grant of certain privileges like those that they had been enjoying in Śōḷamaṇḍalam, for acting on the stage certain plays

---

*Annual Report on South Indian Epigraphy/Annual Report on Indian Epigraphy.

(*kūttu*) at Kāñchīpuram and in all other villages of Toṇḍaimaṇḍalam and who desired these privileges to be engraved on stone in the villages which they visited on their tours.'
(3) *A.R.Ep.*, 1914, No. 65: Kamarasawalli, Tiruchchirapalli district, Tamil Nadu. Tamil. Rājēndrachōḷa I, Year 29.

'Gift of land by the great assembly of Kāmaravalli-Chaturvēdimaṅgalam to Śākkai Mārāyaṇ Vikramaśōḷaṇ for performing the dance (?) *Śakkai-kūttu* thrice on each of the festivals *Mārgali-tiruvādirai* and *Vaigāśi-tiruvādirai*.'
(4) *Ibid.*, No. 253. Tiruveṅgavāśal (Pudukkottai State), Tamil Nadu. Tamil. Vikramachōḷa, year 14.

'Gift of land to a lady for performing the dance called *Sāndikūttu* before the god Tiruvēṅgaivāyal-Āṇḍār, during the festival in the month of Śittirai.'
(5) *Ibid.*, No. 254. Same place. Tamil. Rājādhirāja II, year 5.

'Records a similar (i.e. as in number 253 above) gift of land for performing *Sāndi-kūttu* during the Tiruvādirai festival in the month of Vaigāśi, at the shrine of Śadiruviḍaṅganāyakar set up by Śadiraṇ Irājaṇ *alias* Kulōttuṅgaśōḷa Kidārattaraiyaṇ.'
(6) *A.R.Ep.*, 1917, No. 94: Published in the **S.I.I.*, Vol. X, No. 395 (lines 124-26). Malkāpuram, Guntur District, A.P. Kākatīya Rudrama, Śaka 1183. Sanskrit and Telugu.

Śrī Viśvēśvaradēvasya narttakyō daśa-saṁkhyayā | mukharīdvayā saṁyuktā ashṭau maddala-vādakāḥ ||

---
*South Indian Inscriptions.

ashṭādaśānām=ēteshāṁ pratyēkaṁ sārddha-puṭṭikā |
ēkaḥ Kāśmīra dēśiyō gāyinyaś=chaturddaśa ||

'In the temple of Viśveśvaradēva were ten dancing women and eight drummers including two pipers who received one *puṭṭi* of land each. One Kasmmrian (songster) and 14 songstresses were also mentioned.'

(7) *S.I.I.*, Vol. II, pp. 306-07, Tanjāvur (Tanjavur district, Tamil Nadu) Inscription of Chōḷa Rājēndradēva, year 6. Tamil.

'The immediate object of this inscription is to record that in his 4th year of reign the king assigned a daily allowance of paddy to a troupe of actors who had to perform a drama, entitled *Rājarājēśvaranāṭaka* in the Rājarājēśvara temple on the occasion of an annual festival in the month of *Vaigāśi*. Two years later, in the 6th year of his reign, the king further ordered that his previous donation should be engraved on the stone wall of the temple.'

(8) *A.R.Ep.*, 1915, No. 558: Published in *S.I.I.*, Vol. IX-2, No. 498, lines 36 ff. Cheruvu Beḷagallu, Kurnool district, A.P. Kannaḍa. Vijayanagara Krishṇadēvarāya, Śaka 1436.

'It records that *Karaṇam* Basavayya made a gift of a plot of land in Keriya-Beḷagallu in the division of Ādavānidurga, to the actor Nāgayya, whose father Chāgaya had become famous in the drama called *Tāyikuṇḍa-nāṭaka* and to the actress Pātri, daughter of the Naṭṭuva Timmayya of Pōtavara. The gift was made in the presence of the god for the merit of the king.'

(9) *A.R.Ep.*, 1921, No. 398: Tiruvadi, S. Arcot district, Tamil Nadu. Uttamachōḷadēva, year 14. Tamil.

'Records gift of 96 sheep by Attāmaṉ Ayyāraṉ alias Kaṇḍatōḷ Gaṇḍappayyaṉ of Pūṅguṉram for burning a perpetual lamp in the nāṭaka-śālai-maṇḍapa, erected by him in the temple.'
(10) *A.R.Ep.*, 1925, No. 152: Tiruvaduturai, Tanjavur District, Tamil Nadu. Kulōttuṅgachōḷa, year 46, Tamil.

'Registers a sale of land to the temple at Tiruvāḍuturai by the assembly of Kōṭṭūr alias Jayadara-chaturvēdi-maṅgalam, a *brahmadēya*, which met in the temple of Eḍuttapāda-Viṇṇagar-Āḷvār and a grant of 70 *kāśu*, by Rājādhirājaṉ alias Rājēndraśōḷa-Anantapālar towards the taxes on the land, for the maintenance of a theatre called '*Nānāvida nāṭakasālai*' in the temple.'
(11) *A.R.Ep.*, 1938, No. 48 and also p. 111. Jaṁbukēśvaram, Tiruchchi district, Tamil Nadu. Nāyakas of Madurai. Telugu.

'States that the steps and the *maṇḍapa* were the gift of Vaidyappaya, son of Veṅkaṭēśvaraya, an instructor in the *nāṭakaśālā*' of Vijayaraṅga-Chokkanātha-nāyaka.'
(12) *Ibid.*, No. 49 and also p. 111. Same place, as above. Nāyakas of Madurai. Telugu.
(13) *Ibid.*, No. 216 and also p. 111. Chidipirāḷḷa, Cuddapah district, A.P. Śaka 1501. Telugu.

'References to marionette play and to dramatic art are found in three records of this year's collection. One of these which is in Telugu and comes from the Cuddapah district (No. 216) is dated in Śaka 1501 and registers the endowment of the village Chadupurēla as *sarvamānya* by a certain Chandramayya to one Pedachiṭṭayya for the performance of screen-dramas (*tera-nāṭakam*). The donor, who was probably a local chieftain appears to have been himself an art-connoisseur and composer and an adept in the art of marionette plays as indicated by the *birudas* 'Bommalāṭa-rayitu' and 'Bommalāṭa-Amritakavi' borne by him. The other two records respectively dated in cyclic years corresponding to A.D. 1722 and 1723 (Nos. 49 and 48) are from Jambukēśvaram near Trichinopoly, and refer to the donor of a maṇḍapa as Pāṭakam Vaidyappayya, the son of Veṅkaṭēśvarayya, an instructor in the theatre-hall (*nāṭakaśālāśikshakam*) of Vijayaraṅga-Chokkanāthanāyaka. This theatre was probably attached to the royal palace situated at Trichinopoly. The Madura and Tanjore Nāyaka rulers are known to have been great patrons of music and other fine arts, and the present inscriptions from Jambukēśvaram afford interesting epigraphical confirmation of the encouragements given by them to these arts.'—

(14) *A.R.Ep.*, 1945, No. F 9: Hire-Beṇḍigēri, Dharwar district, Karnataka. In characters of the 12th century. Kannaḍa.

'States that Goravabbeya Chaṭṭiseṭṭi caused to be constructed a *nāṭyaśālā* for the temple of Svayambhū.'

(15) *A.R.Ep.*, 1957-58, No. 497 and also p. 9; cf. *Ep. Ind.*, Vol. XI, pp. 54-55. Jalore, Jalore district, Rajasthan. Chāhamāna of Sōṅgirā-Samarasimha, v.s. 1221, 1242, 1256 and 1268. Sanskrit.

'No. 497 from Jalore is interesting inasmuch as it records the construction of Śrī-Kuvaravihāra by Chaulukya Kumārapāla in v.s. 1221, its renovation in v.s. 1242 at the instance of Chāhamāna Samarasiṁha of Sōṅgirā, the construction of a *toraṇa* for the god Mahāvīra and the hoisting of the flag on a staff made of gold in v.s. 1256 at the behest of the royal family, and the setting up of the golden cupola in the newly built central hall for dramatic performances on the *dīpōtsava-dina* in v.s. 1268.'

(16) *A.R.Ep.*, 1893, No. 534: Published in *S.I.I*, Vol. V, No. 194, 11.6-7. Elūru, West Godavari district, A.P. Śaka 1155. Telugu.

Refers to a grant of land for whitewashing every year the temple *maṇḍapa* and the *nāṭyamaṇḍapa* constructed by the donor, Malya-peggaḍa, son of Śrīman-mahāpradhāni Ananttana-peggaḍa. The temple was of Mūlasthāna Śrī Sōmēśvara-mahādēva.

(17) *A.R.Ep.*, 1905, No. 271: Published in *S.I.I.*, Vol. X, No. 258, lines 46-50. Tripurāntakam, Kurnool district, A.P. Śaka 1134. Telugu.

Refers to the title: *Kavi-ga...vādi-vāgmi-budha-badhira - aṁdhaka - bhaṭa - naṭa-śishṭa-nikhila-yāchaka-jana-chintāmaṇi...*

(18) *A.R.Ep.*, 1905, No. 268: Published in *S.I.I.*, Vol. X, No. 465, 11.91-93. Findspot. Same as above. Śaka 1212. Sanskrit and Telugu.

...Āṭakūṭa-prāsāda-maṇḍapa-nritta-gīta-vādyādi Bharatavidyā-viśārada-naṭa-jan-ōpa-saṅgrahārtthaṁ.

(19) *A.R.Ep.*, 1933-34, No. BK 20: Published in *S.I.I.*, Vol. XVIII, No. 117.1.22. Kāginelli, Dharwar district, Karnataka 1121 A.D. Kannaḍa.

Refers to the construction of the temple of Kāḷēśvarēśa and a *nāṭyaśāle*.

(20) *A.R.Ep.*, 1908, No. 322: Published in *S.I.I.*,

Vol. XIV, No. 254, 1.A2. Kuruwitturai, Madurai district, Tamil Nadu, Jaṭāvarman Śrīvallabha, year 22. Tamil.

This inscription 'purports to have been issued while the king was seated on the *pallikkaṭṭil* called *Pāṇḍyarāyan* in the theatre (*nāṭakaśālai*) within the palace at Madurai. It registers the remission of taxes granted by him in 5 *vēli* of land for worship, etc., to god Tiruchchakkarattāḻvār at Śōḻāntaka-chaturvēdimaṅgalam in Pāgaṉūr-kūrram.'

(21) *A.R.Ep.*, 1899, No. 361: Published in *S.I.I.*, Vol. VI, No. 1142. Simhāchalam, Visakhapatnam district, A.P. Śaka 1190. Sanskrit and Telugu.

It refers to the construction of the *mukhamaṇḍapa*, *nāṭya-maṇḍapa* and *tiruchuṭṭumālya* in the temple of Narasimha on the order of the king Vīra-Narasimha (in Simhachalam).

(22) *A.R.Ep.*, 1895, No. 154: Published in *S.I.I.*, Vol. V, No. 718, 11.3-4. Tamil. Tiruviḍaimarudūr, Tanjavur district, Tamil Nadu. Parekēsari 'who took the head of the pāṇḍya', year 4.

Mentions the *nāṭakaśālai* and stipulates that all the 7 *aṅgas* of the *Āriya-kūttu* should be danced in the temple.

APPENDIX B

VANAJATRA: RELIGIOUS PROCESSIONAL THEATRE

IN the 16th century a unique form of Vaishnava theatre emerged in the Vraj region of north India known for being an ancient seat of the Krishna cult. Operatic in nature it basically depicts childhood acts of the divine cowherd who, according to epics and *Puranas*, spent his early life in the same region.

The Vraj or Surasena region and its association with the cult of Krishna dates back to hoary antiquity. Even Megasthenes, the Greek envoy to the court of Chandragupta Maurya, in his work *Indika*, mentions cities in the region like Mathura and Krishnapura-Vrindavan and the river Yamuna. He also refers to Krishna worship. Inscriptional evidence indicates the existence of theatrical activities in the region which was culturally very rich.

However in the medieval period due to waves of foreign invasions and uncertain social and political conditions the region suffered culturally. Vrindavan wore a deserted look till the 16th century when it started throbbing with activity again.

Initially theatrical activity seems to be confined

basically to *Ras* dances. On one fragrant moonlit night the dark-hued Krishna danced with Gopa girls who looked fair as champak flowers on the white sands of Yamuna. This event in the early life of the Lord manifests deep metaphysical symbolism signifying the union of soul with god. The Vaishnava saints in Vrindavan were deeply influenced by it and they started enacting the *Ras* with the help of child actors in the guise of Radha, Krishna and Sakhis. We find references to this early stage of *Ras* theatre in the *Ain-i-Akbari* of Abul Fazl. The *Ras* stage, a circular dancing arena, came into being at Vrindavan in the middle of the 16th century. With the spread of *Ras* theatre similar *Ras Mandals* were constructed at other places.

Narayan Bhatta, a disciple of the Chaitanya sect, developed the *Ras* theatre and gave it a professional character. It was probably he who added the *Lila* portion to *Ras*. *Lila* means enactment of any episode from the life of Krishna. Now in the *Ras Lila* first Radha, Krishna and the Sakhis dance and after this there comes an enactment of a play based on Krishna lore. In his efforts to dramatise *Ras* theatre, Narayan Bhatta was aided by a dancer named Vallabha.

However the unique contribution of Narayan Bhatta to *Ras* theatre is the concept of *Vanajatra*. *Vanajatra* means pilgrimage to various holy places associated with the life of Krishna. The 16th century Vaishnava saints, particularly of the *Chaitanya* sect, virtually established Krishna myth in the region with great imagination and poetic vision.

For instance they decided that Nandgaon, a small village in the Vraj region was the place where Krishna lived with Nandgopa and his mother Yashoda. The nearby village of Barasana was declared as the place where the beautiful Gopa, Radha, used to stay. They named the narrow lane passing through nearby hillocks as Sankari Khor and it was established that here naughty Krishna would waylay Gopa girls proceeding to the Mathura market with their milk products. They indicated the place *Sanket* where dark-hued Krishna used to put *Kajjal* (collyrium) in the eyes of lovely Radha.

In the *Madhya Lila* of the biographical work *Chaitanya Charitamrita*, it is described how Chaitanya Mahaprabhu rediscovered the pond were Radha and Krishna bathed. Narayan Bhatta's manual, Braja-Bhakti-Vilasa, gives a detailed description of various places connected with the Krishna lore.

Narayan Bhatta associated the pilgrimage to these places with *Ras* theatre and this gave birth to a unique theatrical tradition.

The *Vanajatra* generally starts soon after Janmashtami. The local Panda Sabha makes all arrangements. *Vanajatra* organised by the *Radha Vallabha* sect is famous. The pilgrims walk from one place to another, around six to seven miles a day. The *Ras Mandali*, the company of *Ras* actors, accompanies them. When they reach a particular place the drama is enacted. This drama is based on the story associated with that particular place. For instance at Uchagaon, *Chandravali Lila* is enacted; at Gokul, *Janma Lila* is performed; at Mathura, *Kansa Vadha*

Appendix B

Lila is staged; at Sankari Khor, *Dan Lila* is performed and the Kaliya Daman Lila is performed at Vrindavan.

Vanajatra theatre is a unique phenomenon. The tradition of actually visiting a place of action and presenting a play depicting that action can be claimed as India's unique contribution to theatre. Nowhere else does such a tradition exist. The *Vanajatra* is completed in 15 to 40 days covering a distance of over 100 miles enacting plays at the place of stay. The procession moves, and, with it, the theatre.

The term *Yatra* in the context of the temple institution means festival or festive procession of the presiding deity of the temple. Kautilya in the *Arthashastra* enjoins the officer of the temple administration —*Devatadhyaksha*—to organise *Yatra* and *Samaj* at *Daivatchaitya*, i.e., the temple (5.2). We find the early glimpses of the festive procession of the deities in the rock edict of Emperor Ashoka. Rock edict number five says:

> On account of the practice of dharma by king Priyadarshi, the beloved of gods, there is heard in place of sound of war-drums, the sound of proclamation of dharma, exhibition to the people of Vimana, chariots, elephants, illuminations and divine representations.

Se aja devanam piyasa piyadasine lajine dhammacalanena bhelighose aho dhammaghose vimanadasana hathini agikamdhani amnani diviani rupani dasayitu janesa.

The inscription refers to spectacular processional theatre exhibition of dramatic pageants mounted on chariots and elephants, preceded by fireworks and a troupe of drummers. The words *divyani rupani* may be idols of deities or actors in their guise.

Fa-hien, a Chinese pilgrim who visited India in the 4th century A.D., describes such processions. It came to be known as *Rathayatra*. The oldest sculptural representation of *Rathayatra* of Lord Jagannatha dates back to 8th century A.D., and is housed in the Orissa State Museum at Bhuvaneshwar. Here we find many other sculptural representations of the procession of a later period which are more elaborate in their detail. Elephants, camels, horses and also dancing girls are seen participating in the *Yatra*.

It was a general custom to enact plays during the *Yatra*. The play *Anargharaghava* written by the 9th century playwright Murati was staged at the car festival of Bhagavan Purushottama, i.e., Jagannatha. In the prologue he says:

> *bhō bhō lavanodavelavanālitamaltarukandalasya*
> *tribhuvanamaulimandanahanilamaneh Kamala*
> *Kuchakalashakēlikosturikapatrānkurasya*
> *bhagavatah Purushōttamasya yātrayam*
> *upassthāniyāh sabhasadah ...*
> —Act I

The occasion was the *yatra* of Purushottama who decorates the pitcher-like breasts of Kamala with fragrant musk. The *Sahi Jatra*, street procession, of Jagannatha is also full of theatrical entertainment. The tradition is still in vogue.

We come to know from the prologue of the plays

Appendix B 125

of Bhavabhuti that they were enacted at the time of *Yatra* of Kālapriyanātha at Ujjayani. *Ratha Yatra* is particularly prevalent in south India. Big chariots of wood, sometimes decorated with erotic sculptures, are taken out in procession. However the route of the *Yatra* is not very long and the procession seldom leaves the city or villages. Even if it goes beyond the city limits the distance is not much. But *Vanajatra* is a grand concept, covers a route of about 100 miles, takes full 40 days and during its course nearly the same number of plays are enacted, that too at the spot connected with the theme of the dramatic action. This is something unique in the theatre history of the world.

According to Srivatsa Goswami the purpose of enacting the plays like this is to transport oneself into the space and time of Krishna. The audiences think and feel that they are actually witnessing the episode of Krishna's life in reality. The famous Rupa Goswami who wrote plays based on the Krishna lore and also the book, *Natak Chandrika*, states that the theatre helps the initiate to create within himself love for the Lord. The *Ras Lila* is considered more a religious ritual than a theatre. Through theatre they resurrect the life of Krishna, particularly his early life.

This processional theatre has had a deep impact on yet another Vaishnava theatrical form of central India named *Ram Rila*. In *Ram Lila* the life of Ram is depicted through a series of plays enacted on consecutive days. Each day a particular play is enacted at the locale, depicting the action associated with it.

For instance if the locale is named as Lanka, the fight between Ram and Ravana will be enacted there. In the most famous Ram Lila of Ramnagar the locales are spread over several miles and audiences move from locale to locale along with the play.

But the charm of *Vanajatra* is that Vraj is the area where Krishna actually lived. And the theatrical action takes place at the places directly connected with his life.

APPENDIX C

CHILDREN'S MYSTERY OPERA: RAS

HOW old is children's theatre in India? The *Ras* plays enacted by the children of Vrindavan offer an answer to this question. We know that for at least three centuries plays by child actors have been staged in the Vraj Bhumi. Probably children's theatre originated in India. Acclaimed as the "home of puppet plays", this country may well be called the "home of children's theatre".

The children's theatre at Vrindavan, it is said, originated in the middle of the 16th century. It was promoted by Vaishnava saints like Swami Haridas, Hita Harivamah, Ghamadi Deo and Narayan Bhatta. They recruited children from local families and started enacting childhood *Leelas* of cowherd Krishna at Vrindavan and other adjoining places. The first performance held at Vrindavan was attended by no fewer than 52 kings. However the child enacting the role of Krishna disappeared right before the eyes of the vast audience as required by the story and never returned. The parents viewing the performance were so disturbed that the organisation had to shift their theatrical activities to a nearby village called Karahala. However the atmosphere soon cleared and Vrindavan began vibrating with the plays presented by the child actors.

Ain-i-Akbari, written towards the end of the 16th century by Abul Fazl, one of the nine gems at the court of Emperor Akbar, confirms the existence of children's theatre in the region. The author, who was living in the vicinity of Vraj Bhumi, talks about a class of Brahmins who "dress up smooth faced boys as women and make them perform and sing in praise of Krishna and recite his acts."

One is curious to learn how these children enacted these plays, how they dressed, and what was the level of their histrionic abilities. A detailed account of all these aspects of children's theatre in the Vraj is found in Colonel Thomas Deur Broughton's book, *Letters from a Maratha Camp During the Year 1809*. In his letter of September 8, Broughton describes the Janmashtami festival celebrated in the camp of the Maratha chieftain Maharaja Scindia. Many artistes performed on the occasion but Broughton highly praises the child actors who came from Mathura to present the *Ras* plays. Enchanted by the Indian children's theatre the visiting Colonel writes:

> Both their dancing and singing were far superior to that of common performers, their attitudes were exceedingly graceful and their voices were never raised beyond the natural pitch. Their dresses were appropriate and elegant, especially that of Kunya who wore a brilliant sun upon his head and quantities of superb jewels about his neck

and breast; all of these, as well as the dresses of the other boys, were furnished from the wardrobe of the Muha Raj. After the dances were over, they exhibited in groups statuesque representations of Krishna and his relatives with an accuracy and steadiness quite surprising in such children ... and it was pleasing to see them after the performance, instead of making the usual obeisance, lifting up their little hands, as if invoking a blessing upon the Muha Raj who rose and bowed to each as he retired. We left the tent soon after, highly gratified by the entertainment of the evening.

The Colonel's words bear testimony to the high theatrical standard of the children's theatre. He further informs us that these child actors were especially trained at Mathura and their troupes invited to perform at various royal courts. The eldest among the children would enact the role of Krishna while the youngest was given the role of Radha. Other children enacted suitable roles including that of *sakhis*. This goes to show that at the beginning of the 19th century children's theatre was a flourishing theatrical activity around the Vraj region which includes Mathura, Vrindavan and places around. Frederick Salmon Growse, collector of Mathura district at the end of the same century, refers to children's theatre in the region, paying rich tributes to the child actors.

Many features of this dramatic tradition are unique in the history of children's theatre in the world. The first thing that strikes us was its amazing continuity over the centuries and the high standards of performance. Not only did it preserve old theatrical conventions and styles of performance but also kept the folk music of the region intact. Another interesting feature worth noting is its theme. The child actors of Vrindavan basically depict the childhood leelas of the divine cowherd. Child Krishna is the theme of the children's theatre of the region where Krishna spent his childhood, say the epics and the *Puranas*.

Various reasons are put forward to explain why child actors were chosen to enact the Krishna story. Being pure at heart and still uncorrupted by life they are more suitable to enact divine roles. Though the Radha-Krishna amours have a deep metaphysical significance it is expressed in a highly erotic literary symbolism. While enacting this erotic text there is every possibility of its contents affecting the adult mind, while a child actor under the same circumstances would remain unmoved. Hence the child actor was considered more capable of conveying the non-erotic relationship between Radha and Krishna in its purest form. However some contend that during the changing 16th century social ethos and the political upheaval in the region, adult theatrical activity suffered a setback, hence the introduction of child actors. The most logical reason for introducing child actors however seems to be that since these plays were basically associated with Krishna's childhood, child actors were the natural choice.

Even today despite the waning influence of religion as such, the children's theatre of Vrindavan retains its popular appeal. The number of troupes of 'mandalis' has increased; all of them are constantly in demand. Obviously we cannot ascribe their popularity to religion or religious mythology alone. Audiences are not bound to certain theatrical forms just because of their religious content. Otherwise the tradition of European mystery plays might not have practically come to a halt. It is the intrinsic theatrical merit of the dramatic form which has helped it survive through the centuries.

In its present format the *Rās* musical opera unfolds in two main parts. In the first, which may well be called *Purvaranga*, Krishna, Radha and the Sakhis perform the *Rās* dance. Beautiful patterns of solo and group dancing by children trained in the art by the Samaji or Swamiji who is head of the troupe are also performed. Various folk and classical tunes in different rhythmic cycles are employed to turn the *Purvaranga* into an alluring spectacle.

The second part is the enactment of *Leelas*, that is, episodes taken from the epics and *Puranas* like the killing of the demon Putana, suppression of the ferocious cobra Kālia, teasing the Gopa girls by childish pranks like stealing butter and milk from their houses. The text is prepared by arranging into a neat story sequence appropriate songs composed by poets of the region on the Krishna theme.

A senior person well versed in the various theatrical aspects of the *Rās* theatre floats a Mandali and is known as *Swami*. He recruits good-looking children with excellent musical voices and gives them intensive training. The convention of the *Rās* theatre is to recruit children only from the Brahmin families of the *Vraj Bhumi*.

The remuneration of the child actor varies from

Mandali to *Mandali* and depends mainly on the income they earn. The leading *Mandali* may pay Rs. 400 to Rs. 600 per month for children enacting the main roles. Those playing *sakhis* get paid from Rs. 150 to Rs. 300 per month. The very young apprentice gets quite a low start. If he shows promise he is promoted to more responsible roles. It is the *Swami's* responsibility to provide food and clothing to the child actors on tour.

The education of the child actor suffers however as he has to be on tour most of the time. In the past the *Mandalis* used to employ full-time tutors to educate the children but they are a poor substitute for the present method of school-based education. Hence the saying: 'a boy from *Rās Mandali* and a tonga horse fits nowhere'. After attaining 12 to 13 years of age he is required to retire from the stage. He then tries to remain in the *Mandali* as a make-up man or a musician, or a member of Swamiji's chorus. Many with a good background of mythology and a musical voice turn into *Katha-vachaks*. This means the child who enters the *Rās Mandali* faces an uncertain future.

The *Rās* theatre of Vrindavan is the only professional theatre in the world which depends solely on child actors for the enactment of plays. However the musicians of the *Swamiji's* chorus are adult males.

APPENDIX D

NATYACHARYA

IN the *Ganikādhyaksha Prakarana* of his encyclopaedic work *Arthashastra* Kautilya says:

> Gita vādya pāthya nrutta nātyākshara chitra veena vēnu
> mridanga parichityāgyāna gandhamalyasamyuhānā sampādanā
> sanvāhana vaishikakalā gyānāni ganikā dāsī rangopajīvanischa
> grahayato rājamandalādājīvam kuryāt

The king should arrange for the livelihood of a teacher who imparts the knowledge of singing songs, playing on musical instruments, reading dramatic texts, painting, playing on lute, flute and drum and similar other arts to the girls earning their income from stage appearance, prostitutes and female servants.

The teacher of these arts is known as *Nātyāchārya* or *Nrityāchārya*. His syllabus is given above, however, the full list of arts—64 in number—is given in the

Kāmasutra of Vātsyāyana. His duty was to teach dramatic arts to girls, may they be temple dancers or common prostitutes.

In the early Buddhist literature we find a reference to the teacher of theatrical arts. In *Gamani Samyutta* we meet a dance-master named Talaputa who holds discussion with Buddha about his art. In the *Avadānashataka* there occurs a story of a *Nātyāchārya* of Dakshināpatha who staged a *Buddha Nataka* - a drama on Buddhist theme—at Shobhāvati and also acted the role of Buddha in the play. His daughter Kuvalaya was extremely beautiful. As she tried to entice *Bhikkus* (monks) by the frank exhibition of her lovely figure she was cursed by Buddha.

The heroine of Bhasa's play *Charudatta* whose name was Vasantasena and who was a *Ganika* by profession was trained by her teacher in the art of voice-modulation and stage appearance.

The method of imparting training in dramatics is described in the *Mahābhāshya* of Patanjali. The trainees were taken directly to the stage and were made to observe carefully the senior actors performing thereon. Then they were asked to act accordingly. In his book *India as Known to Panini* Dr. V.S. Agrawal says:

> Patanjali refers to nata teachers of dance—*Ākhyāta*— initiating novices—not through recitation of dramatic texts but by their direct method of taking them to stage.

Some scholars are of the opinion that the Shobhanikas mentioned by Patanjali in the context of enactment

Appendix D

of dramatic episodes of *Bali-vadha* and *Kansa-vadha* are in fact Nātyāchāryas.

In the *Bhāna* plays of the early Gupta period *Nātyāchāryas* are mentioned. The meeting of Vita with the disciple of Nātakāchārya Gandharvadatta named Dardurak who himself was a son of an actress—*Bhāvagandharvadattasya nātakāchāryasyāntēvāsi Dardurako nama natērakah.* He had been to a *Ganika Dēvasēna* to give the copy of the dialogues which she had to learn by heart to act in the play *Kumudvati.* Dēvasēna was supposed to act as heroine Kumudvati. Though she was unwell she accepted the copy because of her respect for the Āchārya—*Āchāryagauravāt pratigruhītam tatpātrakam tayā* (35.13-22). In the same play we come to know that Ganikas used to go to the house of their Acharya for obtaining training in dance —*Āchāryagriham nrityavarena yāsyati* (42.4).

In Kalidasa's play appear two dance-teachers — Ganadas and Haradatta. Speaking about his disciple Mālavika the dance-teacher Ganadas appreciates her quality of learning the things quickly and remarks that it is seldom that one gets such a good disciple. His remark about the clan of Gurus is very significant. He says that the persons who just for earning some money impart training are just like traders—*Kevalajivikāyai tam gyānapanyam vanijam vadanti.* Just as pure gold does not turn black even after putting it into fire, no fault can be found in the performance if training is well given.

Upadēsham viduh shuddham santastamupadeshinah

Shyamāyate na yusmāshu yā kānchanamivāgnishu

Kalidasa has very well portrayed the jealousies and pride of the Nātyāchāryas in the court. The most elaborate description of dance masters occurs in the *Kuttanīmatam* of Dāmodaragupta. Here we meet a very hard task master who makes his disciples tire out during the course of training. A mother of a prospective *Ganika* asks her hunchback female slave to tell the pitiless dance master—

*Kubjē gatva vakshyasi tam nirdayachitanartanā-
cháryam
Hara sukumartanuh kimiti shramamadya karitā
bhavatā*

—Verse 354

(Oh ye hunchback female slave, go to that cruel-hearted dance-master and ask him why he made my daughter labour so much! Her body is very tender as yet, he should know.)

However the most elaborate occasion in the book is the presentation of the first act of the play *Ratnavali* by a Nrityāchārya. It was staged in the temple of Kashi Vishvanātha. We have already seen how frankly he speaks about the present degenerated condition of theatrical arts and how skilfully he presents the play before *Samarabhatta* the prince of Maharashtra.

In *Kathāsaritsāgara* we meet an interesting dance-master Labdhavara who while teaching the queen entices her and runs away with her. This reminds us of Arjuna who lived as a Brihannada dance-master in the harem of king Virāta.

The work *Nrittaratnāvali* of Jayasenāpati gives us a graphic description of a master dancer who is also a dance master. Some of his qualities are:

Kulino nrityashāstrajnya tatvavēdi jitēndriya
Chaturah shishyashishyāyām nartane nipunam swayam
—VII.165:71

He should come from a good family, having good knowledge of the science of dance and himself be adept in the art of dancing and should know how to handle the students under him dexterously and cleverly. Jayasēnāpati prescribes elderly ladies to teach the girls of the royal harem. He says:

Gunairevamvidhairyukta kinchidgalitayauvana
Antahpura strīnām shikshāyām nartakī param
—VII.171

In the various inscriptions quoted earlier, including the inscription of Rājarāja Chola at Brihadeshvar temple, Tanjore, we find dance-masters attached to temples to teach the *Devadasis*. An 8th century inscription at Virupaksha temple tells us about a great actor Achalan, well versed in the technique of Bharata's *Nātyashāstra*. His epithet *Natasevya*, served by other actors with respect, denotes that he was probably a *Nātyāchārya*. According to the inscription he established the superiority of *Bharat-Mata* over other schools of dramatic science (I.A., Vol. X, p. 167). A very interesting panel showing a dance master teaching his *Devadasi* disciples is sculpted on the plinth of the Lakshmaneshvar temple at Khajuraho.

APPENDIX E

SHAKUNTALA SCULPTURES

MAY I fan you with this lotus leaf sprinkled with water. O' beautiful one, place your legs, beautiful and delicate like deep-red rose, on my lap. With pleasure I will massage them!—says Dushyanta to lovely Shakuntala in the third act of Kalidasa's immortal romance *Abhigyan-Shakuntalam*. The sculptor of Bhita froze this lyrical expression in a beautiful sculptured panel. Sheer poetry of his visual image competes with Kalidasa's words!

It was Kalidasa who immortalised the tender love lore of charming Shakuntala whom Goethe later described as a flower of spring. A popular Sanskrit adage about Kalidasa's play says: *Kavyeshu natakam ramyam tatra ramya Shakuntala*, among the literary forms drama is most charming, and among the dramas *Shakuntala*.

For centuries Kalidasa's play has continued to influence Indian classical theatre. It has also nourished the Western romantic taste. The Penguin Dictionary of Theatre, admitting its influence on European drama on its first Western appearance in 1789, states that the play became a rallying-point for romantic taste and reaction against classical canons.

However, it seems, the story of Shakuntala was quite popular in India centuries before Kalidasa appeared on the scene. Vedic literature knew of nymph Shakuntala, mother of Bharat, and of also Dushyanta, though there is no mention of their love relationship. It is the *Mahabharata* which first lifts the curtain over their romance. The folk version of the story is found in the Katthahari Jataka. Kalidasa's *Shakuntala* is created out of an amalgamation of the earlier versions. The addition of romance and lyricism lends it a sweetness all its own.

The Indian sculptors also tried to capture the romance of the story by beautifully depicting it in stone or terracotta. Though they naturally depended on various versions of the love story, being creative artists they improvised, at times adding something of their own to suit the medium they were handling. However, they stuck to the central theme so as not to obscure the identity of the art work.

The earliest sculptural panel depicting part of the story was located in the famous Rani Gumpha cave, near Bhuvaneshwar. It is one of the most beautiful and spacious caves carved in the twin hillocks Udayagiri and Khandagiri. The whole panel is divided into a sequence of three scenes. They are based on the Shakuntala-Dushyanta story and relate their first encounter.

In the first scene we see soldiers standing near a horse. One of them is holding an umbrella, suggestive of royal insignia. In the next scene we see a king

Appendix E

with a fine turban taking out an arrow from his armour, in the other hand he is holding a bow, apparently to shoot the deer running in panic before him. In the background is a tree symbolising the forest. He is King Dushyanta on a hunting expedition. In the third scene we find the king in conversation with a girl poised on a branch of a tree with a deer at her feet. The bow is slung on his shoulder, his expressions changed. He is in the presence of Shakuntala.

The bas-relief dated second century B.C. is close to Katthahari Jataka. According to this Jataka the king met the girl who was collecting wood in the forest. The girl might have climbed on the tree to collect wood. The king gave his ring to the girl as a token of his recognition. In the last scene the girl is seen extending her hand probably to receive the ring from the king. The hunting scene is the legacy of *Mahabharata*.

Shakuntala was a nature-girl, nurtured by the Shakunta birds after she was abandoned by her nymph mother Menaka. Her love for trees and deer is mentioned by Kalidasa. Hence she might have been shown in association with a tree and a deer. The tree-woman motif is very common in Indian art. In the first act of the play Priyamvada tells Shakuntala that when she stands near the Kesar tree she looks like a creeper entwined to it. Was Kalidasa inspired by this sculpture when he wrote these lines?

Two other sculptures depicting the Shakuntala legend have been excavated from the well-known Bhita mound near Allahabad. An interesting terracotta medallion bearing this scene is reproduced in the form of a drawing in the Archaeological Report, 1911-12. The dominant figure here is that of a king in a chariot drawn by four horses. The running deer nearby indicates that the king is on a hunting expedition. A person with outstretched hands is seen standing before the horses, bringing the chariot to a standstill. In the first act of the play, Vaikhanas, an inmate of the hermitage, stops the king in a similar manner. The similarity is extremely striking. In the background is shown Kanva's hermitage. There is a hut among the trees. A girl is shown standing under a tree while another is kneeling by the side of a pond plucking the lotus bud. The sculptor has vividly captured the atmosphere of the hermitage which we find described in Kalidasa's play.

The girl near the tree seems to be watering it. This is how Shakuntala appears on the stage in the first act of the play. The other woman apparently is her friend Priyamvada. Though the figures are not very well defined nobody can miss the similarity of the whole scene with the Shakuntala story as depicted in the first act of Kalidasa's play.

Yet another relief of fine slate, about six and a quarter feet wide, found at Bhita depicts the most tender and lyrical moment in the Shakuntala-Dushyanta love story as visualised by Kalidasa. Though the credit of providing significant and suggestive description goes to Ananda Coomaraswamy, it was Dr. Chhabra who connected the scene on the relief with the Shakuntala story.

To understand the sculpture it is necessary to

Appendix E

delve into its background. After seeing the king, innocent Shakuntala is hit by Cupid's arrow. In the third act we find her resting on the soft bed of flowers along with her friends. She is feeling uneasy. Conversation ensues between her and the other girls including Priyamvada. Shakuntala speaks out her love for the handsome king. Friends advise her to write a letter to her lover. Shakuntala inscribes a beautiful love poem on the lotus-leaf with her nail expressing her tender feelings. All the time, Dushyanta concealed behind the tree is observing everything. Overjoyed by the revelation of her love for him, Dushyanta comes forward.

Blushing profusely Shakuntala tries to get up from the bed of flowers but the king prevents her from doing so. Anasuya requests him to sit on the bed by her side. Friends depart leaving the two lovers together. Shakuntala tries to protest at their departure but the king says:

> Why worry dear, I, your attendant is here to serve you. May I fan you with this lotus leaf sprinkled with water so that you will get cool wind? O' beautiful one, having thighs like an elephant's trunk, place your legs, delicate and beautiful like deep-red lotus, on my lap. With pleasure I will massage them.

The sculptor takes these words of the king as a theme of his art work. Dushyanta is seen here fanning the lovely damsel with a lotus leaf. Commenting on the relief Dr. Chhabra says:

> The turban and the ornament worn by the man do indi-

cate his being a person of high rank, a prince or king. His left hand tenderly touching the reclining maiden is expressive of his appreciation of comeliness of her thighs as also of his readiness to shampoo her limbs, finally the maiden's feet are shown as placed in the lap of the man who is sitting by her side.

This piece of sculpture raises a very significant question. As it dates back to the first century A.D. and is obviously inspired by the play of Kalidasa, can we say that Kalidasa belonged to the first century of the Christian era?

INDEX

Abdur Razak 69
Abhinaya Darpana 4, 27
Adipurana 24
Adya Rangacharya 79
Agni Purana 40, 59
Aitareya Āranyaka 47
Ajanta 17
Al-Baruni 67
Amaravati 17, 55
Andhra Pradesh 75, 101
Anhilpattan 26, 85
Asādhabhuti 20
Ashoka 11, 12, 103
Assam 44, 59, 76, 101
Aupapatika Sutra 35
Avadānshataka 10, 13

Bayana 42, 51, 61, 70, 85
Belur 71
Bhagvanlal Indraji 14
Bhāgavata Purāna 41, 78, 82, 83, 84, 88, 90
Bhagavata theatre 77-89
Bhandarkar, D.R. 12
Bharata 3, 8, 25, 28, 30, 31, 32, 34, 35, 38, 41, 57, 75, 76, 87, 88
Bharhut 17, 55
Bhāsa 78, 79, 102
Bhavabhuti 26

Bhāvashuddha 28
Bhavishya Purana 60
Bhimbetka 5, 6
Bhumra 28
Bhutan 19
Bhuvaneshvar 71
Bloch, T. 53
Brahma Jala Sutta 51
Brihadāranyaka Upanishad 46
Buddha 9, 10, 11, 12, 15, 16, 17, 103, 104
Buddha Nātaka 15
Buddhism 9, 11, 17, 20
Burma 19

Ceylon 19
Chāndogya Upanishad 46
Charja-Pada 15
Chau Ju-Kwa 15
Chidambaram 30
China 19, 112
Chu-fan-chi 15
Chullavagga 10, 54
Coomaraswamy, A.K. 35, 142

Damodaragupta 56, 57
Dasharupaka 27
Dashāvatār 90-102
Desai, Devangana 52
Devadasi 45-76

Dhananjaya 27, 79
Dhar 42
Dīggha Nikaya 9, 10
Dubois, Abbe J.A. 49, 73

Egypt 6, 61

Fa-hsien 13

Garuda Purana 41
Gauhati 59
Gaya 14
Geeta Govinda 71, 85, 86
Gita 28
Goa 100, 101
Gomantak 41
Goswami, Rupa 87
Goswami, Shrikrishnadas 70
Greece 62, 78
Gujarat 101
Gunachandra 26
Guruvayur 44

Halebid 23, 41, 71
Hal Satavahana 82
Harivansha Purāna 8, 37, 40, 80, 83
Harsha 13
Hathigumpha 22
Herodotus 63
Hieun Tsang 61
Hirapur 29, 50
Horrowitz, E.P. 89
Hunter, William 73

Indus 6
I-tsing 13

Jainism 20
Jalore 23

Jātrās 26
Jayasenāpati 39
Jivaka Chintamani 35
Jogimara 53
Jojaldeva 43, 75

Kaiyyata 2
Kalajar 29
Kālidāsa 3, 41, 55, 56, 80
Kāmasūtra 42, 57
Karma Siddhānta 3
Karnataka 37, 64, 100, 101
Karnataka Theatre 37
Karnataka Through the Ages 65
Kāshi 57
Kathā-Sarit-Sāgara 56
Kaumudi-mitrananda 26
Kautilya 52
Keith, A.B. 26
Kerala 39, 40, 41, 101
Kern, H. 16
Khajuraho 20, 41, 47, 60
Khāravela 22
Konarak 41, 61
Konkan 100, 101
Konow, Sten 89
Kopparam 64
Krishnadevaraya 68, 69
Kuchipudi 76
Kumārapāla 23
Kulārnava Tantra 49
Kuttanimatam 56

Ladakh 19
Lalit Vistara 9
Lassen 89
Lenashobhika 66
Levi, Sylvain 18, 19, 89

Index

Luders 54

Mackay 6
Mahābhārata 7, 8, 30, 32, 37, 51
Mahābhāshya 21
Maharashtra 101
Mahavira 20
Mahaviracharitam 26
Mālavikāgnimitram 3
Malatimadhavam 26
Manipur 41, 101
Marco Polo 67
Mathura 13, 19, 21, 22, 54
Meghaduta 55
Modhera 41, 47
Mookerji, Radhakumud 11
Multan 61

Nāgānanda 13
Nagarjunakonda 18
Nandikeshvara 4
Nātak Lakshana Ratnakosha 41
Natarāja 8, 88
Natyacharya 133-138
Nātyadarpan 26, 41
Nātyashāstra 8, 20, 25, 31, 34, 57, 75, 79, 88
Nīlanjana 21
Nrityaratnāvali 39, 76

Orissa 70

Padatadikam 61
Padma Purana 60, 82
Paes, Domingos 68
Palampet 75
Pārijata Manjiri 42

Patanjali 78
Pattadakal 66
Periplus of the Erythrean Sea 61
Pillalmarri 65
Pinda Niryukti 20
Pindar 63
Prabhuddharawhaneya 26
Prasenjit 17
Puri 41, 70, 71, 72, 73
Pushpasena 24

Rai, Rāmānanda 70
Rajaprashniya Sutra 20
Rājarāja Chola 29, 63, 64
Rajasthan 25, 61
Rājatarangini 57, 58, 59, 77
Rajgir 53
Ramabhadra Muni 26
Ramachandra 26
Rama Rao, M. 66
Rāmāyana 7, 8
Ranganath, H.K. 37, 38
Ranigumpha 22
Ranipur-Jharial 50
Rapur 52
Rās 127-132
Ratnagiri 13
Ratnāvali 42, 56
Ravantgiri Ras 25
Rayapaseniya 24
Rhys Davids 51
Ridgeway 89
Rig Veda 32

Saddharma Pundarika 15, 16, 17
Sāhitya Darpaṇa 4
Sanchi 17, 45, 55
Sānkhya 3, 48

Sanskrit Drama 26
Sārangadeva 85
Sariputraprakarana 13
Satyanarayana, K. 64
Shakuntala sculptures 139-144
Shankaradeva 76
Shantala 23, 71
Shatapatha Brāhmana 47
Shilappadhikāram 32, 80, 100
Shiva Purana 51
Shukla, Harkant 67
Sirat-i-Firuz Sahi 72
Sircar, D.C. 14
Sitabenga 54
Sivaramamurthi, C. 8, 88
Skanda Purana 50, 60
Stupa worship 103-112

Taittirīya Brāhmana 7
Taittirīya Upanishad 4
Tamil Nadu 67, 76, 101
Tanjore 29, 63, 76
Tezpur 59

Theragatha 12
Tibet 18, 112
Tiloyapannatti 24
Tirthankaras 20
Tiruparuttikunram 23
Traditions of Indian Theatre 18

Ubhayābhisārika 26, 56, 85
Uttaradhyayana 33
Uttar Pradesh 101
Uttarramcharitam 26
Uzbekistan 17

Vaghli 65
Vājasaneyi Samhitā 7
Vanajatra 120-126
Vasudeva Hindi 22, 36
Vishnuvardhana 23
Vishvanatha 3
Vraj Ka Sanskritik Itihas 25

Wakankar 5

Yagnavalkya Smriti 40